# TESTED

# TESTED

How Twelve Wrongly Imprisoned
Men Held Onto Hope

Peyton Budd

in collaboration with

Dorothy Budd

Photographs by Deborah Luster

Foreword by Craig Watkins,
Dallas County District Attorney

Brown Books Publishing Group
Dallas, Texas

# TESTED

How Twelve Wrongly Imprisoned Men Held Onto Hope
© 2010 MP Books, LLC

Manufactured in the United States of America

For information please contact:
Brown Books Publishing Group
16200 North Dallas Parkway, Suite 170
Dallas, Texas 75248

www.brownbooks.com

(972) 381-0009

A New Era in Publishing™

Hardcover ISBN-13: 978-1-934812-77-8
Hardcover ISBN-10: 1-934812-77-3
Paperback ISBN-13: 978-1-934812-78-5
Paperback ISBN-10: 1-934812-78-1

LCCN: 2010934698
1 2 3 4 5 6 7 8 9 10

This book is dedicated to all the men and women who are wrongly convicted and to those who work tirelessly to prove their innocence. Some will never gain justice, never be released. May these twelve men's stories inspire you to hold onto your hope, faith, and hidden strengths that no imprisonment can destroy.

# Acknowledgments

We would like to acknowledge gratefully the many people who helped make this book possible, especially Jennifer Kinder, whose unfailing belief in the project and bright spirit helped us all get to know these men. We would also like to thank Kristi Leonard, our project manager, who helped us meet all of our deadlines and kept us organized, and Susan Knape, Les Kerr, and Les Baker, who always did everything they could to make this book beautiful. Also, a special thanks to our editors, Kirby Warnock and Dr. Janet Harris, who steered us through the editing process and put up with us with patience and good humor.

Special thanks to Milli Brown and the Brown Books staff who recognized the value of these stories and worked diligently to bring them to publication.

We are eternally grateful to Russell and Kate, whose love, generosity of spirit, and unwavering support made this entire project possible.

Finally, of course, our thanks to the twelve men who shared their stories.

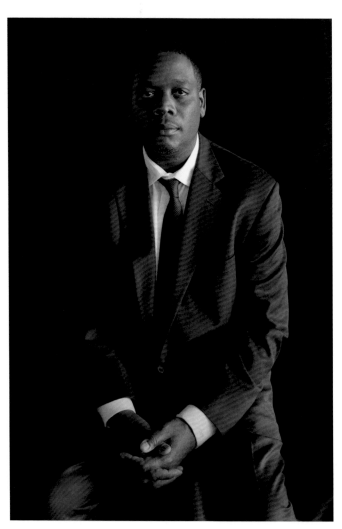

Craig Watkins
Dallas County District Attorney

# Foreword

When I was a seven-year-old child growing up in South Dallas, I can remember sitting in my grandmother's kitchen and overhearing the adults talking around the table. Although I was too young to understand fully, I listened to them talk about a justice system they considered broken. They saw a lot of crimes where the police either didn't respond or behaved as if answering calls in our part of town was a burden, a waste of time. When the police did come, they seemed more interested in checking to see if the witnesses had any outstanding traffic tickets.

My mother's brothers spent time in and out of jail, so we got to experience the criminal justice system firsthand, but we also saw a lot of folks who didn't commit crimes being unfairly taken through the system. So there was this phenomenon of an entire generation growing up with the attitude that you should not get involved with law enforcement—on either side. I was just a child as I watched this take place around me, but I often wondered why no one was doing anything about it.

When I was eight, I went with my best friend, Reggie, to a church service at Christ for the Nations in Oak Cliff. When the service was over, a stranger walked up to me and gave me a Bible he said had been in his family for one hundred years. As he placed it in my hands, he said he believed that I had a calling. At the time, I thought he meant I was going to become a preacher.

I didn't fully comprehend what that calling might be until years later, after I entered college at Prairie View A&M. I started out as an engineering major, but when I took a class in political science, a light bulb went off in my head. I decided to go into public service, and because most public servants were lawyers, I entered law school after graduation.

After earning my law degree at Texas Wesleyan, I tried to get on with the Dallas County district attorney's office but was turned down twice. I got a job with the city attorney, and then went to work with the public defender's office because I wanted to learn how to try cases.

Several years later, I decided to run for district attorney. It was a very difficult race. No one gave me a real chance of winning, but I did. On the day I was sworn in, I had my hand on that one-hundred-year-old Bible given to me years earlier by the stranger at Christ for the Nations.

I came into office a bit shell-shocked; on the first day, they had to show me where my office was located. The attitude around the courthouse at the time was that I was inexperienced ("South Dallas lawyer . . . nobody knows him . . . he didn't deserve it . . . he just rode a tidal wave . . .") so I tried to tread very carefully. Right away I was asked to sign a paper authorizing the destruction of all the evidence from the old cases that had already been tried.

I didn't sign it.

Had I done so, all that evidence preserved over the decades would have been tossed into a trash heap. None of the DNA testing could have taken place, and most of the exonerations described in this book would never have occurred.

Then another thing happened during my first week. A man was exonerated for a crime he did not commit. I went down to the courtroom, shook his hand, and apologized. Everyone found my actions amazing. The news media were all over this story, asking me why I did what I did.

I responded that I was the elected official over the justice system, and the system had failed that man. It was about building credibility and trust. It all went back to that seven-year-old boy at my grandmother's kitchen table.

Not long after that, I received a call from the Innocence Project asking permission to look at some of our old cases. I gave my approval. Then Terri Moore, a prosecutor who had just joined our office, contacted me. She said she wanted me to form a special unit in the DA's office to look into possible wrongful convictions.

"No one else in the country has anything like this," she told me.

I was still new in the office and a bit hesitant to take such a bold step, so I replied that it wasn't time yet.

Terri wouldn't take no for an answer.

"This has been a problem in Dallas for a long time, Craig, and you know it. If you don't do it, it won't get done."

She convinced me, but taking that step was scary because I felt as if I were being tested. Once again, I reached back to what that seven-year-old boy had learned in his grandmother's kitchen. I had mustered the courage to run for DA, but now I needed the courage to do what was right. While I didn't run for office on the issue of wrongful convictions, it was squarely in front of me. I hesitated for a moment, but Terri Moore helped me find my backbone.

We went to the county commissioners and got our funding, then formed the Conviction Integrity Unit. We narrowed the scope to about four hundred inmates who had asked for reviews of their convictions. At the time of these men's trials, the technology to perform DNA testing did not exist. Once the technology became available, we were able to take DNA swabs from the convicted men and compare their DNA to samples in their evidence files. To date, *nearly 50 percent of the cases we reviewed have resulted in exonerations.* In Dallas County alone, we have overturned more convictions than most states. I must add that several of these exonerations were not from DNA testing but from identifying the real perpetrators.

Anyone can look at the religious aspects of this story and see that there must be a reason. Somehow, someone in the DA's office decided to start saving evidence many years ago, and then a DA was elected who wanted to take a closer look at some convictions, then the evidence was saved from the dumpster on his first day in office.

All of this didn't just "happen."

We had to deal with a little pushback because most of the prosecutors and defense attorneys had worked under former District Attorney Henry Wade. Their mentality was that a jury made these decisions and we needed to protect those decisions. However, DNA test results have shown that juries can make wrong decisions, so we must be able to go back and correct those errors.

You probably think you already know this story through its extensive media coverage, from *60 Minutes* to *The New York Times* to the television series, *Dallas DNA.* However, that just represents the headlines. What is sometimes lost is that each and every one of these exonerations involves a living, breathing human being: someone's brother, husband, son, or uncle. Men who, once freed from jail, have had to reenter a world that was advancing rapidly while they remained in a static, unchanging one behind bars.

That's one of the unforeseen challenges—reacclimating them to the "new reality" they will be entering. Those challenges are not always what you think. To put this in perspective, imagine that you fell into a coma twenty years ago in a world with landline phones and television. You then awoke to one with cell phones and the Internet. Now try to envision the friends and relatives who passed away or the children who grew into adults while you were gone. It would be as if your life had been on hold while everyone else's was on fast-forward.

What's next? I believe we need to pass legislation requiring DNA samples to be taken whenever there is an arrest, much in the same manner we take fingerprints. We should also be required to preserve all forensic evidence for twice the length of the sentence. For example, if you are sentenced to thirty years in prison, then the prosecution should preserve that evidence for sixty years. These changes are important for us to move forward and make our system better because whenever we put the wrong person in jail, the real criminal is still out there, committing more crimes. Every time we find the real criminal, we help the victim.

It's time that we have an honest conversation about our justice system, the new tools available, and the hurdles the poor face once they are drawn into that system. This book could make that conversation a lot larger, on a national level, and move us down that road so we don't shy away from the problem or try to make it a racial thing. Exoneration is a first step to justice, but I've seen the challenges these men face once they walk outside the courthouse doors. Fortunately, the Texas Legislature passed legislation creating a compensation fund to offer some measure of redress for the harm these men have suffered.

While no amount of money can ever compensate these men for what they have gone through, by the same token, no news story can come close to conveying the emotional toll they have paid or revealing the faith, hope, or just plain determination that kept them going all those years while they were imprisoned for a crime they did not commit. The biggest surprise to me is that none of them is angry. Somehow they've managed to come out of this with an air of forgiveness, not vengeance, and with their humanity intact.

They have all been waiting patiently, some for more than twenty years, to tell their stories.

You've seen the headlines and watched the television news reports.

Now meet the men behind them.

Craig Watkins
Dallas County District Attorney

Dorothy Budd and Jalah Parker

# Introduction

Every time a wrongfully convicted man in Dallas County was released from prison, I would look at his name and face in the newspaper and search my mind to see if I recognized him. As a former child sex crimes prosecutor for the Dallas County district attorney's office under Henry Wade and John Vance, I knew there was always a chance that one of the overturned convictions would be mine. DNA evidence wasn't available in the 1980s, and eyewitness identification was considered the gold standard. A passing look and a fleeting thought about what it would feel like to spend years locked in prison for a crime you did not commit was all that I gave each man who was exonerated in Dallas County—until I meet Jalah Parker.

Jalah is an African-American woman in her sixties who is several years older than me and lives in a different part of town. We probably never would have met, except that after I left the DA's office I went to seminary and became an ordained deacon in the Episcopal Church. Deacons play different roles in different Christian communities, but in the Episcopal Church, they are ministers of service, especially to the poor, the weak, the sick, and the lonely. One of our primary duties is to pay attention to those people our society pushes into its margins. This means striving to listen to voices that might otherwise go unheard. Our charge for deacons' ordination in the Book of Common Prayer states, "You are to interpret to the Church the needs, concerns, and hopes of the world . . . to show Christ's people that in serving the helpless they are serving Christ himself."

I work as a deacon for The Church of the Incarnation, a large, predominantly Anglo parish located in a Dallas neighborhood that, in contrast to the congregation, is very diverse economically and ethnically. My job at Incarnation is to help our members better hear, know, and love our neighbors. Across a major expressway but within sight of Incarnation's steeple is what remains of one of Dallas's old 1950s-style housing projects, known as Roseland Homes. For more than three generations, it has housed impoverished African-American families. Here Incarnation began a community Bible study as a partnership with Central Dallas Ministries, a nonprofit organization serving Roseland Homes. We met each week to study, pray, and listen to one another. Over time the Bible study grew, and Jalah, who was not from Incarnation or Roseland Homes, somehow heard about it and joined our group.

One evening while we studied the Book of Acts, our discussion question was, "During your lifetime, where do you think you have seen the power of the Holy Spirit at work in the world?" Most people gave examples of things that happened in church, but I will never forget that moment when Jalah raised her hand and shyly said, "Well, for me it was when Craig Watkins was elected district attorney of Dallas County."

I paused for a moment, silently hoping we were not heading into a divisive political or racial topic. When I asked her what she meant, she answered, "Well, we had never had an African-American district attorney, and it really didn't appear people thought he had a shot at actually winning, but he did win. Part of the job of the Holy Spirit is to bring forth God's justice in the world. So the Holy Spirit must have been at work on Election Day. Think about it: If Craig Watkins had not gotten elected, all those innocent men who were sitting in prison all those years would probably have never gotten their DNA tested. They were innocent, but they would never have gotten freedom."

From that moment on, I could not get those men out of my mind. I realized these men had been tested over and over again for years before their DNA was ever submitted to the lab. They were tested in ways I could scarcely imagine. Their belief in the goodness of man and the equity of our system of justice was tested when they were wrongly arrested, identified, accused, tried, and convicted by a system that was far from color-blind. They had their strength and ingenuity tested again and again in prison as they struggled to survive a brutal environment. As the years passed, every relationship in their lives was tested, and many were shattered by the prolonged absence caused by their imprisonment. Their faith was tested repeatedly. No matter how hard they tried or how loudly they cried out for justice, they remained locked up for crimes they did not commit. Even after they were released, the testing did not end. The moment they left prison, more testing began as they faced incredible challenges while struggling to create a life for themselves after being forgotten and institutionalized for years.

I wondered what sustained them. They had languished for years—in some cases decades—in Texas penitentiaries, convicted of crimes that they alone knew they did not commit. Jalah's comment might have remained in the back of my mind, but one day as I walked down the hall of my husband's law office, there was a new picture on the wall. I found myself looking at a small, powerful black-and-white sketch rendered on a jagged piece of paper torn from a small tablet. The self-portrait done by a man in prison had eyes so soulful I could not move past them. Those eyes made me certain the exonerated men I had never met had voices I needed to hear. The next day, I began to try to find a way to meet the innocent Dallas men who had been tested in so many ways.

Like Jalah, I was surprised when Craig Watkins won the election. Usually only experienced assistant district attorneys are elected DA. Not only had Mr. Watkins never been a prosecutor, he was a black man running as a Democrat in Dallas. His opponent was a well-funded, white former DA who had both the endorsement and the campaign war chest of the retiring district attorney. The first time I saw Craig Watkins was the night of his election. To everyone's amazement, he suddenly bounded to the stage late in the evening and was announced as the man who was now Texas's first African-American district attorney.

Four years after he was elected, the words of Jalah Parker caused me to talk to him. After that conversation, I began to feel the scope and enormity of the wrongful conviction issue. Mr. Watkins explained that Dallas was probably not unique in the number of wrongful convictions. It was simply a fluke that over the decades Dallas happened to save and store the evidence needed to run DNA tests. In most cities, such physical evidence was destroyed long ago. I expected one in one hundred of the tests to prove innocence. I was astonished when Mr. Watkins told me that of the cases they selected to test where the DNA was viable, *about half* of the tests proved innocence.

This is not just a Dallas problem. These statistics mean that across the nation thousands upon thousands of innocent people are in prison for crimes they did not commit. It also means the actual perpetrators remain free to commit even more crimes. Now I was convinced that these innocent men needed to be heard, but when DA Watkins agreed to gather these exonerees to speak with me, I had no idea what to expect.

If I were in their shoes, I would be consumed with hate and rage; I imagined them as bitter men.

I was wrong. Nothing could have prepared me for the men I actually met.

I invited my daughter, Peyton, who is a poet and writer, to join me as we interviewed the Dallas exonerees and listened to them. Then she wrote their stories—stories full of betrayal, dashed hopes, and enough irony and mistaken identity to fuel a Shakespearean play. Every man had a legal history impacted by race or class. Each had a chilling story of his life in prison. They endured years of anger and struggled to come to a place of forgiveness. All overcame incredible obstacles to gain their freedom, only to face other hurdles just as daunting after they were released. Yet for all the things they had in common, each man's experience was unique.

After we began to ask them what sustained them, what they held on to in their darkest hours, each man's individuality and faith began to surface. This book does not begin to tell the complete histories of these men. Each has a life that could easily form its own book and a convoluted journey through the legal system that would fill an entire law review journal. This book is not an overview of the legal system or a critique of the structures of society that created and allowed these injustices to occur, although certainly there are books that could and should be written about that.

This book is simply an introduction to twelve amazing men. It is an attempt to listen to and gain a glimpse into what they held onto when they were tested in ways that would crush most people. It is an inquiry into how twelve human beings, trapped in impossible and unfair situations, somehow made a way where there was no way. Whether what strengthened them was faith in God, faith in a loved one, faith in a part of himself that each was forced to discover, or simply faith in his own unquenchable desire to survive until the day he would somehow be proven innocent, each clung to something different as he was tested.

Faith sustained all of these men, but as we talked to them, it became clear there was often something more than simply believing what they relied on or thought was true before they were incarcerated. What they faced was so overwhelming that each man had to reexamine his beliefs and discover new truths about himself, and God, to endure. For some, like Eugene Henton, there was a striking conversion to a new faith. Richard Miles and Entre Nax Karage returned to, reinterpreted, reexplored, and recommitted to the faith they grew up with. Others, like Johnnie Lindsey and James Giles, developed their own innate gifts, graces, and talents to their full capacity.

The title of each chapter is a word that conveys what each man found to hold onto. While most of us will never face what these men have withstood, we are all tested in ways that threaten to overwhelm us. In our own moments of testing, we can be strengthened by the examples of these men.

I am grateful that Jalah Parker's prophetic words caused me to do more than glance at some names and pictures in the newspaper. What I learned from these remarkable men tested me in ways I never expected.

Their stories can inspire anyone facing a test in his or her own life. However, to give the reader fair warning, although there is a startling sweetness about almost every man, these are not sweet stories. The exonerees will inspire you and break your heart at the same time. That these men found something to cling to does not reduce them to simple stories of faith and triumph.

Every single man lost something that can never be restored. That is the reason the Dallas exonerees not only inspire us but also compel us. Their powerful stories invite us to reexamine and reevaluate many of our prejudices and preconceptions. Billy Smith, whom you will meet in this book, issues the invitation this way:

"When you get convicted for something you didn't do, and hear that gavel hit and hear the words 'we find this man guilty,' and you do time, whether it's a day or a week or a year or twenty years, that takes something. It takes a bite out of you. The only thing I ask is that you just look. Don't just look at the surface; see if you can look in the heart."

Reverend Dorothy Budd

Johnnie Lindsey

Billy Smith

Steven Phillips

James Giles

Richard Miles

Entre Nax Karage

Christopher Scott

Thomas McGowan

Victor Thomas

Eugene Henton

Keith Turner

Stephen Brodie

High school track star

Convicted and
sentenced to life

1983

In 1981 *a young woman riding a bicycle on the White Rock Lake trail was attacked and raped by a shirtless young black man. Police never found her attacker, and the case went unsolved. One year later, police arrested Johnnie Lindsey for the attempted sexual assault of a woman on the same trail. Although he acknowledged he was at White Rock Lake the day of the attempted assault, Lindsey insisted he did not commit either offense. After being photographed by the police without his shirt, Lindsey was chosen by the victim from a photo lineup. He was charged with both attacks and sentenced to life in prison. Nearly twenty-six years later, a DNA test on semen taken from the 1981 victim proved his innocence. He was released September 19, 2008.*

# Johnnie Lindsey

**INCIDENT DATE:** August 25, 1981

**WRONGFUL CONVICTION:** Aggravated Rape

**AGE ENTERING PRISON:** 30

**AGE LEAVING PRISON:** 56

**WRONGFUL TIME SERVED:** 26 years

*Diagnosed with colon cancer*     *Exonerated*

2008

# Music

Johnnie Lindsey's world is full of music. He sits on his porch and listens to the sounds of life—traffic, construction, voices—and what he hears is music.

The first thing you notice when you meet Johnnie is his smile. Then there is his wardrobe. From the hat cocked at the perfect angle on his head to his glistening shoes, his clothing is impeccable.

Couple those with Johnnie's big, soulful eyes and his melodious voice, and you can easily imagine him as the lead singer for an R&B band, moving confidently across the stage. When he looks up slyly at you and hits you with that high-beam grin, he's like Snoop Dogg posing for an album cover. It's a curious disconnect because Johnnie's pleasant demeanor and upscale footwear reveal no hint of his rock-hard past.

Even though Johnnie was always a talented musician, he never got to pursue that path fully. The truth is, although he always had music in his soul, for part of his life Johnnie Lindsey was no choirboy.

"I guess I was about ten years old when my dad died. And after he died, my mom, she had a nervous breakdown, so she had to be committed to a mental institution. I was practically raised by my grandmother and my aunts."

Despite a difficult life at home, Johnnie had both talent and promise. Early on, it looked as if he had the world by the tail. In 1969 and 1970, he was a star for the track teams at Booker T. Washington and North Dallas high schools, earning all-district and all-state honors. He was good enough to earn a track scholarship to nearby Southern Methodist University.

He also liked to sing. His grandmother took him every Sunday to the Greater North Park Church of God in Christ, where he often sang hymns with the congregation.

In high school, he formed his own group, The Magnitudes. They sang "Oh Happy Day" and "Ain't No Mountain High Enough." In their matching black pants and gold shirts, The Magnitudes managed to take first place at the State Fair of Texas talent competition.

"I should have been a singer," Johnnie says. It's the only hint of regret he allows to slip from his lips.

Somehow things got off track, and he took a wrong turn. When Johnnie arrived at SMU, he immediately "got distracted" and fell in with a party crowd. The late nights and easy access to drugs eventually got the better of him, and he dropped out of school.

Once out of college, he says, "I got in with some bad people."

It all started after he ran into an old high school acquaintance who was "going down another route." They went to have a drink, started hanging out, and pretty soon, "one thing just led to another."

He began to hang with an even rougher crowd, dealing drugs, stealing credit cards, or "working the hustle," as he calls it.

Remarkably he still held down a full-time job. That was just like Johnnie. Even in elementary school, he made enough money mowing lawns in the summer to pay for all of his school supplies and clothes as well as his sister's.

"I believe in work," he says. "I've always worked because I figured that if it wasn't going good, then I had money from my regular job to fall back on."

Unfortunately his luck soon ran out.

He was sent to prison for three years for robbery. That experience scared him so much that he vowed he would never do anything to be sent back to prison again. After his release, he found a job at a commercial laundry.

One night, after a fight with a girlfriend, Johnnie left the house. He stayed out all night, drinking and driving around Dallas, not thinking anything significant would come from an evening of nursing a broken heart.

The next morning as he watched the sun rise over White Rock Lake, he thought to himself that he should have been in church, but instead Johnnie was in the wrong place at the wrong time. A series of rapes had occurred along the White Rock Lake trail, and a woman who jogged past him that morning accused him of attempting to assault her.

On the strength of eyewitness testimony, he was convicted of two attacks, even though he had pay stubs and time cards showing he had been at work. He admits that his prior robbery conviction didn't help him much.

"Even my own court-appointed attorney straight up told me, 'You're an ex-con, and you are going back to prison.'"

He was handed a life sentence to be served in the Ellis Unit of the Texas Department of Criminal Justice at Huntsville. In 1982, the Ellis Unit had the distinction of housing violent offenders and every prisoner on Texas's death row. The one-time high school track star and singer described it as "the diagnostics of hell," explaining that the guys there would kill you "for a nickel, a penny" or possibly less. He survived, but his method of survival was a process.

During those first few months, he watched death row prisoners take the long walk to the execution chamber and said he was glad just to be alive. He repeatedly told himself, "Where there is life, there is hope, and at least I am alive."

For a while, this mantra got him through the day, but as time went by, he slowly sank into a deep depression. He started to sleep more.

"You don't hear nothing down there. All you hear is that 'bam' of the doors opening and closing and people yelling and screaming and saying 'get off that' or 'get out here,' but you never hear the sounds of life."

One day while watching the World Series in the rec room, he couldn't take it any longer. He trudged back to his cell and began to cry; sobbing uncontrollably, he pulled his blanket over his head. As he drifted off to the temporary peace that sleep provided, he heard a voice say, "I will save you."

He thought he was hearing things in a depression-induced stupor or losing his mind, but somehow that voice made him feel better.

"Whenever I felt like I was at the end of my rope, I'd just think about that voice."

The next morning, he decided to stop lying in bed all day and start looking for an outlet, something he could do. It wasn't long before he discovered that the Ellis Unit had a prison band and music reentered his life. He auditioned and was accepted.

"There was a lot of guys that come in, wanting to get in the group, that couldn't. And it was sort of like a prestigious thing, you know."

From that point on, he looked forward to the band's Friday night jam sessions and weekend gigs "like a kid waiting on Christmas."

"I always got nervous before every performance," he explains, "but by the end of my time, I was one of the oldest guys in the band. I was one of the 'originals' and that represented something."

Time cards showing Johnnie was at work at the time of the rape, and his sex offender registration card.

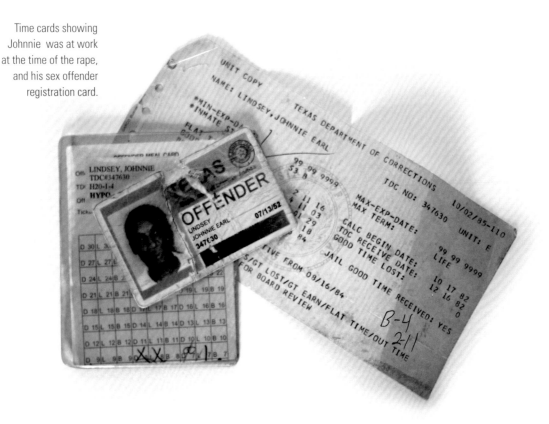

He sang at every weekend church service, "even the Muslim ones." Sometimes the prison chapel would be standing room only with "a couple of hundred people wedged into it." It didn't matter, as long as he got to sing.

Another way to combat depression was work. His previous experience at the commercial laundry helped him land a good position in the prison laundry. Always a hard worker, Johnnie moved high enough up the ladder to where he was allowed to perform alterations and repairs for the prison officers. In the ensuing twenty years, he never missed a day of work. Johnnie worked hard and was liked and respected by his coworkers, particularly the laundry captain, Cynthia Johnson.

This made him a good candidate for parole.

To improve his chances, Johnnie purposely steered clear of trouble. Whenever his fellow inmates made fun of him for his squeaky-clean record, he would just grin and reply, "Hey, it's not easy being cheesy, but I try."

But there was a problem.

At his parole hearing, the board insisted that Johnnie issue a statement of contrition declaring he was sorry for what he had done. He balked, saying he could not show remorse for a crime he never committed.

"They said I was being stupid, and all I got to do is tell them I'm sorry. I told them I was sorry for what happened to the woman, but I didn't do nothing."

He was not only denied parole, but he also had to wait another three years before he would even be considered again.

Adding to his disappointment was the fact that he didn't feel well. He had become increasingly nauseated and endured multiple symptoms that were diagnosed as a stomach ulcer. After enduring months of suffering without any relief, Johnnie collapsed in his cell. He was taken to the infirmary, where for three days he lay on the verge of death before he was bused to the hospital in Galveston.

Johnnie was dying of colon cancer.

Lying alone in the prison wing of the hospital in Galveston, Johnnie willed himself to die. "The cancer hit me, and it was rough. So I just lay in the hospital, and I said to God, 'I'm ready to go, I'm trying to make my peace and I'm ready to go.'"

He concentrated every ounce of strength he had left in his weak and thinning body and asked God to take him away from this life of pain. Then he heard a voice he had not heard for twenty years once again say, "'I will save you.'"

And he held on.

He survived the surgery, healed, and returned to Ellis. "It felt like coming home."

He had now been incarcerated so long that prison had become his home and his family. Cynthia Johnson, the laundry captain, was especially kind. Even though he was too sick to work, she insisted Johnnie come and interact with everyone at the laundry so he wouldn't be alone in his cell. Cynthia had seen sick men become isolated and die in prison. She also allowed him to make some button-up shirts after she noticed the surgery made it difficult for him to pull the standard prison top over his head. He was beginning to feel like himself again, just in time for chemotherapy—eleven rounds of it. He was moved to a unit closer to the Galveston hospital.

"They would pump so much in me that by the last day of each treatment I was like a sick dog, lying in a corner somewhere."

During this time, he returned to his music for help. He gave concerts for himself, singing every song he could remember in that cold, dark hospital room in Galveston.

"Then I started looking at my distasteful situation, and I found a little beauty, just little spots of beauty in it. And those are the things I sort of cling to, to keep me going day to day. I'd find it in a blade of grass or when I was singing. When I was singing, I was just being alive, I was just being alive."

Two months after Johnnie finished his chemotherapy, he was contacted by public defender Michelle Moore and told he was being considered for DNA testing. "Right when I heard that, I said I'm going to go pack my clothes because I'm fixing to go home."

Then he had a revelation. Now, after twenty-six years, he knew what the voice had meant earlier. Johnnie was saved. He was saved from the dangers of Ellis, saved from cancer, and saved from himself by a higher power that knew Johnnie needed this time to become the man he is today.

In the visitors' room, Michelle handed him her cell phone to call his sister with the good news. "I said, 'Michelle, I don't know how to use this.' That's how long I had been gone."

In 2008, Johnnie Lindsey was finally released from the Texas Department of Criminal Justice's penal system with a full apology from not only the judge but also Dallas County District Attorney Craig Watkins. As hard as this may be to understand, Johnnie's years in prison have not left him bitter. Here's how he explains it:

"Looking back at my life, at how I used to be, I was running here and running there. I left destruction everywhere because I didn't care. Then God came into my life, and He set me down, and then He sat down by my side, and He said, let me show you how your life should be. When I look at the way I am now versus the way I was before this happened, I'm glad I had more time in. I wasn't ready. Going through this experience alone, it got me ready. By the time I was exonerated, all of the anger and hostility was gone. I was just ready to see my mom."

Johnnie pauses and sighs. "It's sad that I see so many people living in a prison out here. It's unbelievable, if they just knew what I've been through. If they could just go in there and experience a fraction of what I have, then life wouldn't be so bitter out here. Some people are free, but they're still locked up. We can create prisons for ourselves out here. Just live your life!"

Now Johnnie listens to the world. For more than two and a half decades, he didn't hear a baby cry or a car honk. He lost his chance to become a famous musician, but maybe he has gained something better. Johnnie can hear the music that is constantly shaking and celebrating the world around us, the music that most of us are too self-centered or busy to hear.

*Arrested for robbery*

*Convicted and
sentenced to life*

1986

In the *laundry room of an apartment complex, a woman was approached by a man with a knife. He dragged her to a grassy field and raped her, then fled. The victim told her boyfriend immediately afterward and said that she thought the man lived in the complex. They went to the apartment of Billy Smith, where the victim identified him as her rapist, and then called police. Despite an alibi provided by Smith's sister, who testified that she was at home with Smith at the time, he was convicted of rape based on the victim's eyewitness testimony and sentenced to life in prison. On December 13, 2006, he was exonerated after DNA testing proved he was not the rapist.*

# Billy Smith

| | |
|---:|:---|
| **INCIDENT DATE:** | August 7, 1986 |
| **WRONGFUL CONVICTION:** | Aggravated sexual assault |
| **AGE ENTERING PRISON:** | 35 |
| **AGE LEAVING PRISON:** | 54 |
| **WRONGFUL TIME SERVED:** | 19 years, 11 months |

*Conversion to Islam*                    *Exonerated*

2006

# Serenity

*"God grant me the serenity to accept the things I cannot change,*
*courage to change the things I can, and wisdom to know the difference."*

—*Reinhold Niebuhr*

Billy Smith exudes an air of majestic serenity. It makes him seem regal. With his salt-and-pepper beard, his elegant demeanor, and a voice that is soft but still full of power, he conveys the calm dignity of a lion at rest. But the Billy Smith you see today is a very different man from the Billy Smith of 1986. When he was thirty-five and thrown into prison, he was not particularly majestic, and he was not remotely serene. Back then, he was a guy who liked to fight, and he was mad.

He had a lot to be mad about. He had already been to prison once for burglary. That made him tough, but it didn't make him particularly mad. He had done the crime, and he did the time. The second time was different—he was innocent, and this time he was furious.

On August 7, 1986, Billy was sound asleep in the apartment he shared with his sister when a policeman came to the door. He remembers walking out onto his second-story balcony: "It was barely morning, and the sun was just beginning to shine. It was a beautiful morning, and the wind was cool and fresh. I had never seen a morning like that before, and I have never seen a morning like that since. Never."

In the midst of all this beauty, something not so beautiful was about to unfold. A woman he had never met pointed up at him from a squad car in the dim parking lot below. That was the last morning Billy Smith enjoyed as a free man for nineteen years and eleven months.

Billy wants the world to know that what happened to him during his years in prison is more than just a story. "This is not my story. This is my testimony. It's a testimony to God's goodness and His mercy and to the fact that God has forgiven me. It's a testimony that through all these things that I did in my life, I was able to know God, and to find God and His love and His care and His protection."

This is how he feels today, but on the day he entered prison. his feelings were entirely different. What he felt then was anger, defiance, shame, and confusion. He was angry because he had been sent to prison based on flimsy evidence and sentenced to life for a crime he did not commit. Once he arrived, he was so defiant he refused to work or cooperate in any way. For two years, he was on restriction, segregated from the general prison population. He spent most of his time brooding in his cell. He was ashamed of what he had been charged with. Rape was abhorrent. A rape charge was so shameful that during his first three years in prison he never told anyone his conviction charge. He was confused, wondering how this had happened to him.

"Wasn't a day that passed that I didn't question, why. Why did I get found guilty? And I didn't have one single human being on Earth I could ask why."

He spent so much time pondering this alone that sometimes he even doubted himself. There were moments when he feared that maybe, somehow, what they said about him was true. Although he had absolutely no memory of the crime, he found himself wondering whether he really had raped that woman.

His attitude and circumstances led to depression. Billy believed that being in prison was like enduring the trials and tribulations of the prophet Jonah. He was trapped in the belly of a great fish with no way to escape, and he feared it might crush him. He was trapped in prison, and none of his family ever visited. He was alone and seemed to have no reason for hope.

But two things happened. The first inmate he shared a cell with was a Muslim who had a copy of the Quran. Even though he had been raised a Christian, Billy began to read the Muslim holy book. He became curious about Islam. His second cellie had a cousin who was involved in a prison correspondence ministry, and she began to write to Billy. Although he had never met her and never would, Billy believes, "God put her in my life. I have never even seen her, but I will always be grateful to her. God speaks to us through other people if we just pay attention."

Billy wrote to her, saying he didn't understand why all these things had happened to him and that he felt abandoned by God. She replied that perhaps God had not abandoned him—maybe Billy had been running away from God. Maybe God needed to put him somewhere where he could not run away, a place where he would be forced to sit still and listen. Her letters comforted him, but his feelings of depression and isolation continued to grow. After two years in prison, he was at a breaking point.

As he sat alone in his cell one night, he began to consider taking his own life. He spent hours on the edge of his bunk, staring at the floor, contemplating dying. His thoughts began to whirl together, but in the silence, something emerged. Out of his sorrow and confusion, the words to a prayer he thought was somewhere in the Bible began to repeat themselves over and over in his head. It was actually from the Serenity Prayer recited at every Alcoholics Anonymous meeting. Over and over Billy said those words. "God grant me the serenity to accept the things I cannot change, and the courage to change the things I can."

As the night wore on, he made a mental list of all the things he could not change. It was a long list.

He could not change that he had been wrongfully convicted of a rape he did not commit.

He could not change that his family never visited and barely wrote.

He could not change that no one had ever once called him or put a dime on his commissary card.

He could not change that the years of his life were ticking by as he sat stuck in jail.

He could not change that he had a life sentence.

He could not change that he was confined to an ugly nine-by-five-foot cell.

At first, the list just made him even more despondent and increased his resolve to die. But he still kept hearing those words, "Grant me serenity . . . give me courage to change." At last, in total exhaustion, Billy began to drift off to sleep.

Suddenly a new idea came to him. "In spite of all the things I can't change, there is still one thing I can change—me. That's the only thing I have control of—me."

Instead of killing himself that night, Billy Smith fell asleep. He was still confused, but somehow he also felt strangely comforted. When he opened his eyes the next morning, he resolved simply to put his right foot forward, and that is what he's been doing ever since.

"I got up the next morning, and my foot hit the floor, and I said 'I'm going to do it like this. I'm going to start out on my right foot.'"

He quit fighting. He worked his way off restriction. He entered the society of the prison around him but steered clear of its many temptations. He took a job. He started going to school. He began to go to the prison library to work on his case. He started reading the Quran and began going to Islamic classes and chapel services.

He was both surprised and comforted when he discovered that the Quran contained an Islamic version of the tale of Jonah in the belly of the great fish. But he found more than comfort. In Islam, he found structure.

"I completely changed my way of life. I started looking for ways to stay out of prison while I was still in prison. I became disciplined. I came into prison rebellious, like a teenager, but now I wanted to be an adult. I wanted to come out a responsible person, someone with some character and some integrity."

Change didn't come effortlessly. There were habits developed over a lifetime that would have to change. The process was not easy, but in the teachings of Islam he discovered an approach that worked for him. He learned that if you want to change something in yourself, and find it hard to change, you must do it in steps.

"First you decide to change the thing. Then you change it with your mouth and with your words. Next you change it with your hands. If you can't change it with your hands, then you change how you hold it in your own heart. If there is nothing else you can do, you do the only thing you can. You move to hating that thing in your heart. When you have done all that, and there is nothing else you can do, you give it over to God. That's when you begin to change."

Billy *did* change, and people noticed. He first realized he had made changes when other inmates stopped avoiding him or trying to fight him and began to come to him for advice. How he experienced prison began to change gradually. Instead of driving him to the brink of death, prison slowly became different. It got to the point where in spite of everything that happened, he will tell you that he had a good life in prison. It was good because there he began to learn the discipline of his religion. "God gave me enough time to change."

In his remaining years in prison, Billy often prayed he would not serve his full life sentence, and he didn't. In 2001, he first heard of DNA testing and applied, but his request was denied. He had to wait three more years to reapply. When at last he was accepted, a bench warrant brought him back to Dallas so a swab of DNA could be taken from his mouth.

He got the news that the test results proved his innocence while he was standing in line at the commissary. He was handed a letter, opened it, and began to read. When he got to the part that said he was going to be freed, "I laid my head on the back of the brother's shoulder in front of me and just started crying. That was the first time anybody in prison had seen me cry. It was the first time I showed the soft part of me. When the brother in front of me asked what was wrong, I told him, 'I'm going home, man; I'm going home.'"

The great fish that had swallowed him so long ago was finally going to spit Billy out. The experience had held him and changed him, but it had not crushed him. He was fifty-four years old when he was finally released from prison. He believes that through DNA testing, God answered the prayer he uttered from inside the belly of the fish. "I served nineteen years and eleven months, but I didn't serve life."

Billy Smith's story of life in prison ends with his exoneration, but his testimony goes on. His hard-won serenity is his testimony.

"Even if you have been a certain type of person for so long, when you are ready to make a change and you actually admit in your mind that you are ready, you *can* change. And don't say it can't happen overnight because I am here to tell you it did. You can start to make a change. You can go to bed one night and get up the next morning a different person. You can just get up the next morning, and you can start working on it."

"You can start to make a change.
You can go to bed one night and get
up the next morning a different person.
You can just get up the next morning,
and you can start working on it."

Penny Baker watches
the basketball game

Convicted and
sentenced to 30 years

1984

**Dallas police** *were on the trail of a man who was entering gyms, spas, and apartment complexes, forcing women to disrobe at gunpoint, then engaging in various sex acts. Semen from one of the attacks was collected from a rape victim after an assault in her North Dallas apartment in front of her two-year-old son. The victim chose Steven Phillips as her rapist from a police photo lineup. Despite an alibi, Phillips was convicted of sexual assault and sentenced to thirty years in prison. He was released on August 4, 2008, when the Innocence Project submitted his DNA for testing and proved conclusively that another man in a Texas prison had committed the assaults.*

# Steven Phillips

**INCIDENT DATE:** May 14, 1982

**WRONGFUL CONVICTION:** Aggravated rape

**AGE ENTERING PRISON:** 26

**AGE LEAVING PRISON:** 50

**WRONGFUL TIME SERVED:** 24 years

*kes Coffield Bulldogs basketball team*

*Becomes newspaper editor*

*Exonerated*

2008

# Swagger

Steven Phillips's eyes are green.

His warm smile is complete with a small gap between his front teeth that fits perfectly on this boy from Arkansas.

Not particularly big or tall, Steven still manages to exude a presence of strength and power. And behind the rectangular lenses of his glasses, his eyes are green.

Somehow, despite more than twenty women vehemently claiming that their attacker had piercing blue eyes, Steven Phillips was tried and convicted for a series of brutal rapes and assaults he did not commit. During the investigation, one officer tried to point out, "He doesn't have blue eyes," but the lead investigator said, "They're blue enough."

Before this run-in with the law, Steven had lived a good life. Born in Texas, he spent most of his childhood in Arkansas. "My stepdad was living the Arkansas dream. He was a paint contractor. Mom was working at the grocery store and everything, raising a bunch of kids."

Right about the time they moved to Arkansas, Steven discovered a love for sports.

"I know the very moment it happened. There was a girl named Penny Baker in the fourth grade with me. I was playing pee-wee basketball. I was runnin' down the court, and mom says I got my shirt on backwards and wrong side out. I threw the ball up like this, and it actually went in. I was amazed. When the game was over, Penny Baker was with her friends, and as I walked by, she said, 'Good game, Steven.' I was hooked."

After that, sports became an integral part of Steven's life. He played basketball all through high school, and when he was sixteen, he learned he had a wicked left jab.

"I won the district Pine Bluff AAU and regular Golden Gloves."

He was one of the few "white guys" boxing in his district and went on to win a state Golden Gloves championship.

At age seventeen, he joined the army. "I did four years in Germany mostly. I saw Europe, and it was all over then."

As you talk to Steven, you can't imagine that he spent twenty-four years in prison on a false conviction as a serial rapist. His description of life before prison sounds just like the story of anybody else you might know and love.

In 1982, a massive hailstorm hit Dallas. Fresh out of the army, Steven followed the hail damage with his new job as a roofer. He also had a young wife he met in the service who was about to have a baby. Things were going well, but after living in Dallas for a month, Steven was arrested for a misdemeanor and had his photograph taken. A week later, in an article describing a search for a serial rapist, his face and name were in the Dallas papers as a suspect under the word "Wanted."

Steven describes having to drive around the roadblocks set up to find him so he could turn himself in at the downtown police station. "In my naïveté, I believed that I was going to get hung up there for a day or two . . . maybe a few days or whatever, until they got this thing cleared up and figured out. It did not turn out that way."

The case brought against him involved a two-day crime spree where a hooded man assaulted more than twenty women in North Dallas health spas and apartment complexes. Dozens of women were molested, and several were raped. Steven was put into a six-man lineup, but there was something wrong with the one-way glass. He could see through it. Instead of watching the victims being brought in one at a time, he saw a group of women on the other side.

"It was crazy. I'm number four in the lineup, and you can see they are in there with the cops, and they are all having this open discussion about number four. Some are looking at me and going like this, shaking their heads, 'No,' but then the cops say something, and another victim from the health spa comes in. She comes up real close to the glass, and as soon as she sees me, she starts crying, and I'm going 'oh, my gosh, man.' Then I see several more identify me."

At his trial, he believed that once the victims saw him face to face they would realize their mistake. The early testimony gave him some glimmer of hope because they talked extensively about the attacker's eye color. The witnesses started off certain about the man's eye color, but eventually they wavered on the stand.

"They went from 'I'll never forget those eyes. Those piercing blue eyes, I'll never forget them,' to, 'Yeah—I think they were blue.'"

Much like the detective, the jury thought his eyes "were blue enough" and found Steven guilty.

"So they convicted the wrong guy. What about all the victims? After they said, 'Let's just go with this guy,' the real guy is out there committing crime after crime."

In prison, Steven's powerful left hand saved him more than once. "I was twenty-six, a pretty strong guy, plus I got a good left jab. Saved my life."

He didn't win every fight, but he won enough so the other men noticed. "Oh yeah, my good friend Anthony says I walked down the hall with a swagger. I don't know about that, but honestly, I don't look behind me because I don't screw over anybody. I do the right thing, so I don't need to look behind me. Also, I got that left. They kinda knew about that too."

Aside from the fighting, the moment Steven arrived at Coffield he got involved. Maybe that's why in spite of everything, Steven was able to decide "I'm living my life. I'm in prison, I'm not dead. I'm living my life."

The first thing he did was start school. He enjoyed taking classes because he liked getting to talk with the professors. It meant escaping the institutionalized world, even if it was only through conversations about philosophy and existentialism.

Steven also renewed his love of sports. In the mid-1980s, the Texas prison system had traveling sports teams that went from prison to prison to compete. At Coffield, the most esteemed sport was basketball. The Coffield Bulldogs were famous, they were good, they were tall, and the entire team was black.

"These were like college-level players, getting above the rim . . . that high."

But Steven had a plan.

"I kind of cheated to get on there. I wrote a request to the guard who served as the Bulldogs coach. It read, 'I'm a white guy, about six feet, six inches, 240 pounds, and an all-state champion.' So they called me to try out. There were about a hundred guys there, and they were looking for this giant white guy. I walked in and the coach asked, 'Where's the big white guy?' I said, 'That's me,' and he just started to laugh. I had tricked him, but I bluffed my way in, he let me try out anyway, and I made the team."

Steven also played for the Coffield football and softball teams. "In prison, sports is really something."

There is one softball game he always remembers. "I'm twenty-six years old, and I'm on the top of my game. I'm playing shortstop, and I'm racing across, picking up the ball behind second base, flinging it over to first, and it's just a play like you can imagine a major league ballplayer making." Playing sports made him feel free.

"You know what I think gave me some strength? Every day I'd wake up and go, 'I'm innocent. Still in prison, but I'm still innocent.' Honestly, I think that gave me a little power, a little something to look forward to, just knowing I'm innocent."

About five years in, Steven became aware of a feeling that every prisoner eventually experiences. "You are going along, serving your time, when all of a sudden it's like . . . thunk! You're there. You're not going anywhere, this is where you're at, and the reality of that really comes home."

One August, he took that feeling with him on an unair-conditioned trip to solitary. He spent fifteen miserable, humid days "just sitting there sweating like a pig," with nothing in his cell but a few cigarettes he managed to smuggle in and the only thing you can legally have in solitary—a battered copy of the Bible. Steven decided that on top of working and being a three-sport athlete and student, he should start reading his Bible again.

"I was baptized in the Church of Christ when I was fourteen, but since then I'd been to Amsterdam, more than once."

Reading his Bible in solitary was a step in the right direction, but it did not transform him into a perfect Christian. "It wasn't like, 'now I'm a Christian, and I don't have any more sin in my life.' Nothing like that. I was still smoking, contraband, fighting, pornography, whatever. I crossed all kinda boundaries, but there was something there, there was something going on there. I wanna tell you right now I didn't have it all together, but as my faith grows, my understanding grows. I started to see that sin might be fun, but you had better be careful with that. It will diminish you."

Through his newfound study of scripture and eventual church attendance every Sunday, Steven found yet another thing to do. He became a newspaperman, reinstituting the monthly *Sons of God Chapel News Bulletin*. Every week he would sit in his newsroom.

"I'd just go into my cell with my old Royal typewriter, and I'd put it right on the shitter. I'd have a white, two-gallon bucket that I'd sit on, and I'd blast that bulletin out. I would take maybe four hours to get it lined up just right. I would just thoroughly enjoy it—something worthwhile."

Even though the chapel bulletin was supposed to contain religious content, Steven managed to work in his other passions. He included pieces about the sports teams, and every month he had an article that highlighted a prisoner's artwork. He started getting other inmates to write articles. Soon he was making more and more photocopies of each issue, and the whole prison was reading it.

Throughout his entire imprisonment, Steven was working on his case, but things weren't going that well. In 2001, a law was passed that prisoners were entitled to DNA testing. He applied in 2004, but the judge denied his request. Shortly afterward, Steven made a trip down to the prison hospital in Galveston to have his green eyes checked.

"I'm just looking out the bus window, nobody next to me now. It's amazing. I'm looking out at the peninsula, and I see the sun over the waves and everything. It's high tide, it's choppy, and it's like a million sparkles, like a million possibilities on the horizon, but at the same time, I know that I had lost that appeal and that I was done."

When he got back to his cell at the unit, all of his belongings had been removed. He couldn't get his possessions back until morning.

"There's nothing in my house. It's empty, like an empty tomb maybe. And I knew that it was over with. I had been doing everything *pro se*, trying to do it all by myself. Suddenly I knew that *pro se* would never win, ever. So I prayed. I said, 'Help me, Lord, with your strong right hand. Help me because I cannot do this by myself.'"

The typewriter Steven used as the editor of the Sons of God Chapel News Bulletin.

Steven Phillips could do almost everything: he could fight, he could play sports, he could study, he could write, he could put out his own newspaper, he could read the Bible, and he could live his life, but without God, he could not get out of prison.

"I believe that was the key right there. When you really give something to the Lord, it does not matter which way it goes; you are going to be good with it. I think that's what you're after right there. From that moment forward after that prayer, I did not file another writ—nothing. I shoved the typewriter up under my bunk, and I did not get it back out."

Steven had won a thousand games and his fair share of fights, but he had never won a legal battle. "I had never won anything *pro se*, not even one time. No motion, no writ, no anything. Zero. So I gave it to the Lord, and since that moment, I have never lost a motion, a writ, a hearing, ever. Not once."

In 2008, his request for a DNA test was finally granted. Steven was exonerated. He is still living his life, but it's a little sweeter now that he's out from behind bars. His strong arms are tanned from a fishing trip to Arkansas with his son and his new wife, Connie Jean. The sparkle is slowly returning to his green eyes, and he probably still has a wicked left jab.

He just doesn't need it anymore.

Makes $30,000      Convicted and
per year      sentenced to 30 years

1983

In 1982, *three armed men entered the home of a Dallas couple. While one man robbed the husband at gunpoint, the other two raped the wife. The three men then took her to a grassy field where they all raped her repeatedly. The victim was five months pregnant. A month after the crime, the victim identified James Giles from a lineup after learning his name. He was convicted for a gang rape and sentenced to thirty years. He was exonerated in 2007 through a combination of DNA testing and the victim's admission that she could not positively identify him as one of the attackers. The real rapist was a neighbor of hers.*

# James Giles

**INCIDENT DATE:** August 2, 1982

**WRONGFUL CONVICTION:** Aggravated sexual assault

**AGE ENTERING PRISON:** 29

**AGE LEAVING PRISON:** 39

**WRONGFUL TIME SERVED:** 10 years, 14 years on parole

*Released from prison*

*Owns several profitable businesses*

*Exonerated*

1993

2007

# Hustle

James Giles was born to hustle.

He was raised in Geneva, Texas, where there is nothing but "backwoods and squirrels." His father was a chicken farmer with eleven kids to feed. From an early age, they all learned how to "work the coops."

"The chickens had to be kept a certain way in the summertime. You'd have to let 'em out of the chicken houses and go outside. We'd let them outside the coop in the hay field, and then we'd pull them back up at night. We'd have to wash the feed troughs and keep it rolling all day long." It was hot, backbreaking work.

James had a momma who could sell anything. She would lend out a stick of butter and get back two and sell East Texas moonshine like nobody's business, even though she was a God-fearing, Christian woman.

"My momma didn't drink, but she sold the hell out of home brew, which is that homemade beer."

In elementary school, James got into trouble for stealing the other kids' marbles, but he wasn't actually stealing; he was winning them in playground games of "keepsies" and penny-pitch matches. "You gotta learn this stuff. I learned it through the course of having hard times."

Hemphill High School didn't become integrated until 1968, but that didn't stop James from becoming the quarterback of the school's football team. As he recalls, "If I couldn't call the shots, I wasn't going to play." He also played basketball and ran for the track team. He reckons that through these high school sports, he began to realize what he had—the ability to read people, assess a situation, and benefit from it as much as possible.

James moved to Dallas with a cousin in the mid-70s to see if he could make it in the big city. It turned out he sure could. After holding down several jobs, he began a three-year apprenticeship in the Carpenters' Union. By 1979, James Giles was "on top of the world"—happily married with a new baby boy, a beautiful house in the suburbs, and a $30,000 yearly income.

Then in 1982, "all hell hit the fan."

A woman was brutally raped at gunpoint by three black men, one of them named James *Earl* Giles. She was five months pregnant. Shortly afterward, three white detectives showed up at James *Curtis* Giles's doorstep, twenty-five miles away from the scene of the crime. James had just arrived home after a day's work and was lying on the ground playing with his three-year-old son while his wife was cooking dinner.

"They tell me they have a warrant. I said I really don't know what you're talking about, I know it's a mistake, but man, I don't know what's going on. I call back to my wife to call a lawyer because I don't know what this is. So anyway, I go on and get in the car with them."

Had anyone told him he wasn't going to return for more than ten years, he would have laughed.

For six months, he sat in county jail awaiting trial, but James was not the kind of man to just sit and wait. He was always working and watching. As soon as the jailer locked the holding cell door, James began to hustle. The minute his wife put $50 on his commissary card, James became a businessman in jail. He made loans to other prisoners whose wives and families weren't as devoted or as fortunate. If an inmate didn't have any money in his account, James would get him a bag of coffee, but once the prisoner's money arrived, he owed James two bags. One fellow named Red came to James again and again for commissary loans.

During his time in jail, James says he wasn't concerned. "I'm not worried. I didn't know nothing about it, so nothing to worry about. As far as I was concerned, it was all a mistake. So we went from there. I'm trying to find out what's going on, day after day, trying to get it cleared up. After five, everybody goes home, everything will be clear tomorrow, tomorrow, the next day."

"The next day" didn't come particularly soon.

At James's trial, both his wife and his mother testified as alibi witnesses. His wife explained that James was definitely at home at the time of the rape because he never missed *Gunsmoke* and *Solid Gold* on Sunday nights. His mother testified that James always called her every Sunday after church and that day was no exception. In addition, James's lawyer questioned why the victim never mentioned James's gold-capped teeth, when they clearly were an incredibly prominent feature. The jury could even see them shining from across the courtroom.

On the first day of deliberations, the jury was out until 11 p.m. with a vote of seven to five in James's favor. The next day at 3 p.m., he was found guilty.

James Junior waves to his daddy.

"The guilty verdict never bothered me," says James. He swore to himself, "This is not gonna hold because I am going to find out the truth if it's the last thing I do." However, there were moments when James was discouraged. After the verdict, the bailiff kindly allowed James to say a final good-bye to his three-year-old son. In a small holding cell to the side of the courtroom, he held James Jr. as they both broke down.

"Then it was just emotion. I just cried a lot, and James is scared to death and he starts crying. So the bailiff comes and gets him and takes him back out."

Shortly after his arrival at the Coffield Unit, he learned that his son had been diagnosed with sickle cell anemia and might not live past the age of five. Again, going against the odds, James chose not to give the diagnosis much thought because he believed his son would live a long and happy life.

A few bits of luck did follow him into prison. His old buddy Red was transferred from Dallas County to Coffield that very same day and still owed James $40. Somehow James Giles had managed to come into what he describes as the toughest prison in the system with somebody owing him a favor. At Coffield, James watched a lot of men turn into "punks." Some of them looked like big, strong guys. He realized right away that in prison, just as in life, it's not your size that determines your power; it's your mind.

"It's just a mind thing" is an expression he uses repeatedly.

As soon as he looked up Red, James Giles was back in business. He began to rise in status as one of the many prison loan sharks, controlling the underground market of commissary goods, like ground coffee, tuna, noodles, and postage stamps. He also

Handcrafted
Bible covers made
by James in the
prison craft shop.

participated in the thriving world of prison gambling where inmates bet on anything from dominos to what's for dinner or who is going to win the Super Bowl. James knew how to gamble, but he also understood human nature. He knew the odds, he knew the personalities, and he knew that to win consistently, you had to have an eye for every last detail.

This was nothing new. "I've been gambling *with* my life, *for* my life, *all* my life."

Another piece of good fortune arrived a few years later. One day as James stood in the commissary line, he heard someone call out the name Marvin Anthony Moore. At first, he couldn't remember why the name sounded familiar, but then it clicked. Although James had never laid eyes on him, Marvin Anthony Moore had been listed as one of his codefendants at the trial. Now here he was, standing in line in front of James.

After pulling a few strings, which was easy for a guy like James, he was able to arrange a visit with Marvin and ask him what he knew about the case. Then he found out about James *Earl* Giles, a man with a similar name who was the real rapist. *There were two James Giles,* and somehow the system had charged, tried, and convicted the wrong one. This new information would help exonerate him some fifteen years later. In the meantime, he remained in prison, certain of his innocence but unable to prove it.

As the years passed, the inmates began calling him "Sergeant" Giles, then "Lieutenant" Giles. Finally the whole unit, even the guards, recognized him as "Captain" Giles.

"First, just one or two people called me Captain Giles, but then pretty soon everybody called me that," he recalls. "You work your way up in the ranks. If you get the respect of everyone, you learn you can do pretty much whatever you want. Everything is built around relationships. Once you build those relationships in the system, no one is going to mess with you. After you've built your reputation, you can kind of lie back, but until then, you gonna have to work for it."

Hard work was something James Giles was never afraid of, especially if it yielded a profit. In those first few years, he relied on the money his wife dutifully sent to him every month; however, as a born entrepreneur, soon James was actually managing to earn money for his family while behind bars. He began to use the craft room and ordered tools and basic leatherwork items to make beautiful wallets, clutches, coin purses, belts, and Bible covers from exotic hides such as ostrich and crocodile. He then sent these handcrafted leather goods to his wife, who sold them at their church. Around the holidays, he even took custom orders and hired four or five inmates to help him produce items to send to Dallas in time for Christmas.

Despite his success, James explains, "You are never happy in prison, no matter what you are doing—playing basketball, watching a football game, or even eating a good meal. There is never a good day in prison. The only good one is the day you leave."

After ten years, James was granted parole. All he could think about was his family. His wife had stayed with him and brought their son to visit every weekend during the entire time he was behind bars. Now he was coming home. As soon as James was released, his brother drove James to his house. He strode up the front walk, but when he reached the front door, a locked screen door barred his way. Stunned, James listened to his wife tearfully explain that he must leave. She wouldn't even let his son, now thirteen, come outside to greet him.

"She handed me my stuff through the door."

What James didn't know was that while he was in prison, the Texas Legislature passed a law that required those convicted

James Giles's business card.

of sex crimes to register as a sex offender. He was not permitted to come within three hundred feet of minor children, including his own son. When his wife learned about the law, she decided she could not live like that and filed for divorce. After waiting ten years for their reunion, James was not even permitted to live under the same roof with his family.

True to form, James didn't let the sex offender registry stop him from seeing his son or making money. He sneaked visits to see James Jr. whenever he could and returned to working construction. He also became an ordained minister. Wearing his new clerical collar to an automobile dealership, he talked his way into a great deal on a new car—with no money down. He continued "hustling," even starting several businesses. Today, he owns a barbecue joint, a life insurance company, an income tax preparation service, and a bail bond company.

"If you think you can do better than me, then pick it up and walk with it," he says with no apology.

In 2007, he was finally exonerated through years of hard work and a dedication to revealing the truth. Today, James is doing what he was born to do—hustle. His business card displays his face smiling at you from the center of a "million-dollar" bill, and his cell phone is rarely silent.

"I believe in me more than anything. I have to. Because it wouldn't even make sense for me to cut myself short of what God blessed me to do.

"You can't have faith in God unless you have faith in yourself," he declares emphatically. "You're born into this world, and you got to work for everything you get. You got to hustle. Nobody is going to give you anything, but when you become a God-fearing man, there is no limit to what you can do. I can do anything a hand can do for a man."

And he does.

Every waking day.

*Leaves home a*
*begins dealing d*

In 1994, *someone fired a 9mm handgun into a car at a Bachman Lake gas station, killing one man and leaving another permanently disabled. On the strength of an eyewitness account, Dallas police arrested Richard Miles, who denied being at the location the evening of the shootings. Richard was sentenced to forty years for murder and twenty years for attempted murder. Working on Miles' behalf, Centurion Ministries, a prisoner advocacy group, discovered a police memo that identified the real shooter by name. The information had never been provided to the defense. Based on this new information, Richard Miles was released on October 12, 2009. He was the first man freed in Dallas County in a case that did not involve DNA evidence. He is currently attempting to be granted a full exoneration.*

# Richard Miles

**INCIDENT DATE:** August 15, 1994

**WRONGFUL CONVICTION:** Murder and attempted murder

**AGE ENTERING PRISON:** 19

**AGE LEAVING PRISON:** 34

**WRONGFUL TIME SERVED:** 15 years

*Convicted and sentenced to 40 years plus 20 years*

*Step-father's death    Released*

1994

2009

# Masks

*"No man for any considerable period can wear one face to himself and another to the multitude, without finally getting bewildered as to which may be the true."*

*—Nathaniel Hawthorne,* The Scarlet Letter

Richard Miles is a chameleon.

Throughout his life, he has worn many masks to blend into different environments. He's worn the mask of a church boy, a drug dealer, and a prisoner, but as Richard says, "You can tell a chameleon he's a dog, and he might be able to look like a dog, but he knows he's a lizard. At the end of the day, a chameleon always knows he's a lizard."

Behind his mask and technicolor skin, Richard Miles is a good son and a good man.

Ever since he was a small child, Richard hated going to church. The problem was his stepfather was the bishop of his family church, God's Holy Church. That meant they attended church four times a week without fail. Richard can still tick off the days: Sunday mornings, Sunday evenings, Monday evenings, and Wednesday evenings. At his house, skipping church was not an option—there was no getting out of it. However, there was one part of church Richard didn't mind.

"I liked going because I played the drums. So all the females—well, they used to like me. So we didn't have a boring church, but as I grew older, I saw my friends and they'd be going out, starting their young lives, and I felt like I had started to become stagnant."

Church provided about the only interaction with girls he was allowed. The rules at the Miles's household were pretty strict: all had to be home by seven o'clock; they weren't allowed to talk to girls on the phone; and they were forbidden from attending school dances and events.

"I was like fifteen years old, and I was sneaking in the back room talking to a girl on the telephone. My mom picked up the phone, so I hung up real fast, but I forgot that once you pick up one line, even though you hang up the phone, that the call doesn't end. So I walked out of the back room, thinking I was all right, and then I hear my mom on the phone saying, 'Baby, I don't know why he hung up. Why'd he hang up in your face?'"

Strict rules weren't the only thing that irritated him. Even though his dad received plenty of respect on Sunday mornings, there were things about him that made Richard cringe with shame.

"My dad was a disabled veteran, so he couldn't really work, but what he did was he 'scrapped,' and oh, that irked me, because, man, I felt like it was degrading. We'd get up early in the morning in the summertime; we'd get in the old truck, and we'd go around the neighborhood looking in people's trash cans for stoves, hot water heaters, and aluminum. Then we would take it to South Dallas and sell it."

As Richard got older, he began to envy people he thought had a bit more freedom and a bit more flash.

"I remember being on the church bus, and you see someone pull up next to you in a nice car, lots of jewelry—you say, 'Man, they got it made.' You want to put yourself in their position."

So when Richard was seventeen years old, he had a conversation with his father he will never forget.

"Me and my dad was sitting in the van, He was just telling me, 'You know, if you can't fully accept the rules and regulations of the house, you can just leave if you want to.' I took that and that's what I left on. It was sort of like a crossroads at that point in my life, and that's when I physically, spiritually, and mentally went in a totally different direction."

He didn't even make it one day, falling quickly into the rough world of life on the streets. He saw a path he imagined was a lot more glamorous than "scrapping" and "churching" every weekend, so he took it. In no time, he was selling drugs and living the life of the guys he had seen through the church bus window, but he was no happier—the life he adopted was just another mask.

"It was demanding on the streets. You don't really have any friends. The rules of the street are if you're not hard, you got to play like you're hard. This phase of my life, I call it October 31. Every day was like Halloween. Everyone was dressed up in these crazy costumes and seemed to forget that at some point they were going to have to take them off and go back to who they really were."

He began to realize that life on the streets wasn't as glamorous as it looks in the movies.

"I'd have to sleep in my homeboy's garage when I didn't produce enough finances to get a hotel room, or whatever, and there were nights when I put my life in jeopardy just being in a particular environment."

Richard had come full circle; he had the flashy façade of the prosperity he'd once envied. All dressed up and driving in a fancy car, he would think, "I'm in this car and the church buses are driving by. That's when I have a flashback. My lifestyle now, it looks good, but it's not what I want it to be, and I'm wondering if someone, some young kid, is looking at me, at this vehicle, and saying, 'Man, I'd like to be him.'"

About then, Richard was picked up by the police for drug possession and sentenced to five years of probation.

On a hot August night just a few weeks later, as he was walking from one friend's house to another, he decided to stop at the liquor store for a drink. As he left and crossed the street, "A helicopter comes over the top and it's shining its light down, and I said, 'They're looking for somebody.' Then all of the sudden, it's like out of nowhere all these police cars just come from everywhere, and they jump out and say, 'Get on the ground, get on the ground! Where's the gun?'"

When Richard was taken to the police station, he says he didn't feel scared because he knew he could call the people he was with that night to corroborate his story. They did, but still a detective came into the room where they were holding him and said, "Your story checks out, but you killed those people."

The hardest part of that night was calling his parents.

"Not because I was afraid they'd be mad at me, but just the fact that they are ministers, and now their son is locked up for one of the most heinous crimes a person can ever commit, taking another person's life. How will society look at my mom and dad with the thought that I killed somebody?"

To make things easier on his parents, Richard put on a different mask in jail—a happy mask. He wore that mask every time they visited. He always tried to convince his family that he had everything together, but in reality, "On the inside, I was tore up and didn't understand anything.

"You can't never be all right when you're locked up—you just have to appear that you are."

Richard was sentenced to forty years plus twenty years in a Texas prison with no chance of parole until he served half his sentence. When he heard this, he put on yet another mask—the mask of a fighter.

"I guess I would call it my survival mask. You see, that's the tactic of the chameleon—the ability to blend into any environment or situation to prevent yourself from being harmed. I believe that's one of God's gifts that He allowed me to have."

Even though Richard had lived as a dealer and might have seemed tough on the streets, he knew his toughness was a charade.

"You got to realize, I didn't grow up in a violent-type environment. I don't know how to fight. I've never been in a fight in my life until I got locked up."

In county jail, there were several older inmates who had been to state prison.

"Some of the older cats in jail, they began to teach me how to box. They used to wrap up our mattresses and take our sheets and ball 'em up and wrap 'em so we'd have a punching bag. They would show you how to wrap your sock around your hands and teach you how to fight and teach you the etiquette of prison."

They also tell the kids that once you get to prison, you've got no choice if a guy talks down to you: *you have to fight*.

After Richard learned some basics from the prison veterans, he thought he was ready. "Before I left the county jail, I was sparring a lot, and I told myself, man, I'm looking good." He soon found out that in the Texas pen, a new guy needs more than a few boxing lessons and a little swagger.

At the Coffield Unit, Richard's first real fight was "one for the books."

"I was sitting in the dayroom, when he came in there, and just out of the blue: Whap! Just went off on me. Now everybody's looking at me. And this is prison, so you can't have nobody just disrespect you and call you all types of ungodly things because now it's a stage. You have to perform. So I get up and I say, 'Man, you know what? I'm not going to let you disrespect me. We might as well take this to the back.'"

The beating was bad, but the worst part was who beat him.

"Yeah, I remember Bushwick. He was a midget. He was probably about four-foot-eleven and had tattoos on his face. Also, he had real stumpy arms. One of his arms,

Necklace made in the prison craft area with Richard's favorite Bible verse: "I can do all things through Christ who strengthens me." Philippians 4:13

I think it'd been shot, so you could see where the skin was grafted. I guess he didn't have any feeling in it because that was the hardest arm I ever felt, and he used it like a club.

"Lord, this little man tore me up. Oh, Lord Jesus, I'd never gotten beaten up so bad in my life."

Although he lost the fight, Richard had proved to the unit he would punch back, and that was all that mattered. "Now you have your card, your get-by-free card, in prison because you had that fight."

Richard didn't like fights, so after that, he avoided them and slowly fell into the regular prison routine, but he still hated being there.

"I was always looked at and looked upon as something I wasn't, and that just used to kill me. When they told me to walk on the right side of the hall, I walked on the left. I never viewed myself as an inmate because I didn't do what they said I did. I'm not a convict or a criminal; I'm forced to be in prison. But it wasn't me."

Because he didn't consider himself a criminal, Richard tried to associate with what he calls "free world people"—the nurses in the infirmary, the workers in the library, and the teachers in the prison school system.

"I didn't want to have to talk to bosses all day or inmates," he explains, "because their mentality is just so short."

He started attending school and began to read his Bible and cherish the scriptures. Strangely enough, in prison Richard began to lower his mask and discover who he really was.

In a haunting echo of Nathaniel Hawthorne's quote from *The Scarlet Letter*, Richard says, "At some point from point A to point B, when you put on so many masks and take off so many masks, you begin to lose your own self-identity. So I have to understand who I am now and just embrace who God has made me to be."

As he began to understand who he was, his relationship with his father began to change. "Our relationship started to blossom while I was in prison. I was growing up, coming of age. I was starting to understand life. I knew that I could become the son he wanted me to be."

His mom and dad visited every week, and on those visits when they weren't discussing scripture, Richard opened up to his father about things that had happened in the past.

"He would always know where my friends stayed. He would stop right in front of one of my friend's houses and start going through their trash. I'm like 'It's already bad enough that we're scrapping, but do we have to stop in front of Jeremy's house?'"

Once Richard confessed to something his father could hardly believe. Richard said that one morning he was so embarrassed that his father was planning to drive him to school in the noisy, old scrap truck full of broken microwaves and sewing machines and all manner of junk. He went into the house, got a knife, and "accidentally put some holes in the truck's tires." He sat stone-faced and innocent-looking as his father went outside, saw the truck, and came back in hollering, "Jesus! Jesus! Somebody put every one of my tires on flat!"

Richard was now grown up enough to realize that scrapping wasn't degrading.

"All it was to my dad was an honest way of providing a livelihood for us, but I hadn't looked at it that way.

"I think we accepted each other's faults and advantages. He knew that I loved him and he loved me, and he knew I was innocent."

Sadly, Richard's dad never got to see his son released. In 2008, his father stopped visiting. He was diabetic and had been diagnosed with cancer.

"This big dude, who used to lift up refrigerators, he'd come to see me at the end, and he was smaller than a girl. It was crazy, like I'd seen him shrink right before my eyes, and it hurt that I was not able to be there with him and comfort my mom as she went through this time."

Richard's dad died six months before his son was released from prison.

Christopher Scott, who was in prison with Richard, explains what it was like.

"Part of the conditions of life in a Texas prison is that when you hear them call your name to come to the chapel you know immediately one of your relatives has died," he says, shaking his head. "It's the longest walk you'll ever make."

On the day Richard's mother came to tell him the news, he had to put on a mask—the mask of the strong son, who would protect and support his newly widowed mother.

"I sat there and I cried. I thought I've got to fix myself, got to get my mask. I pulled my mask on, but I think I left half of it in the office, because I broke down for a little bit."

It was the only time his mother ever saw him cry.

"I wasn't allowed to go to my father's funeral so it wasn't really until the Sunday after the funeral when it really hit me. I used to write my mom and dad every Sunday. I would listen to gospel music, sit down with my cup of coffee, and start my letter with 'Dear Mom and Dad,' but that particular Sunday I couldn't start the letter with 'Dear Mom and Dad.' That's when it hit me."

Richard was released in October 2009. Unlike the other men in this book, he is not yet exonerated. Although he was found innocent and released from prison due to prosecutorial misconduct, he has not been exonerated by the State of Texas, and therefore has not received any compensation. He must deal with the intense difficulties of rehabilitating into society without any money. His situation gives him a unique perspective.

"Being out is harder than being in.

"Being in, everything is handed to you. Prison makes a person want to rely on something and not rely upon themselves. They tell you when to wake up, tell you when to go to sleep, tell you when to eat. You're not a human being; you don't know how to function as a human being. Yet when you're released, society looks at you to be this competent, law-abiding, tax-paying, well-adjusted being, and you're not."

Since his release, Richard has started studying business management at Eastfield College. He works nights at a Hilton Garden Inn to pay for school and help out his mom. With the help of his lawyers, he also continues the fight for full exoneration. Richard is in yet another environment and wears yet another mask.

He started working as a youth minister at his father's old church and finds himself again at a crossroads. The assumption is that eventually he will take his father's place as the pastor, but now Richard is being careful. He's still a chameleon, but he's not going to play any new role until he's sure it fits who he truly is.

"Right now I am still trying to understand myself and life. To be the pastor would be totally inappropriate. It would be like a sheep trying to lead more sheep. So for now, it's not the thing for me."

Once again, Richard will have to discover who he really is. When asked what people would see if they saw him without a mask, just the real Richard, he hesitates and thinks carefully before he answers. "I think if I took off the mask, you'd see a strong-minded, strong-willed, happy individual. I like to think of myself as a comedian, and people *do* say I look like Jamie Foxx."

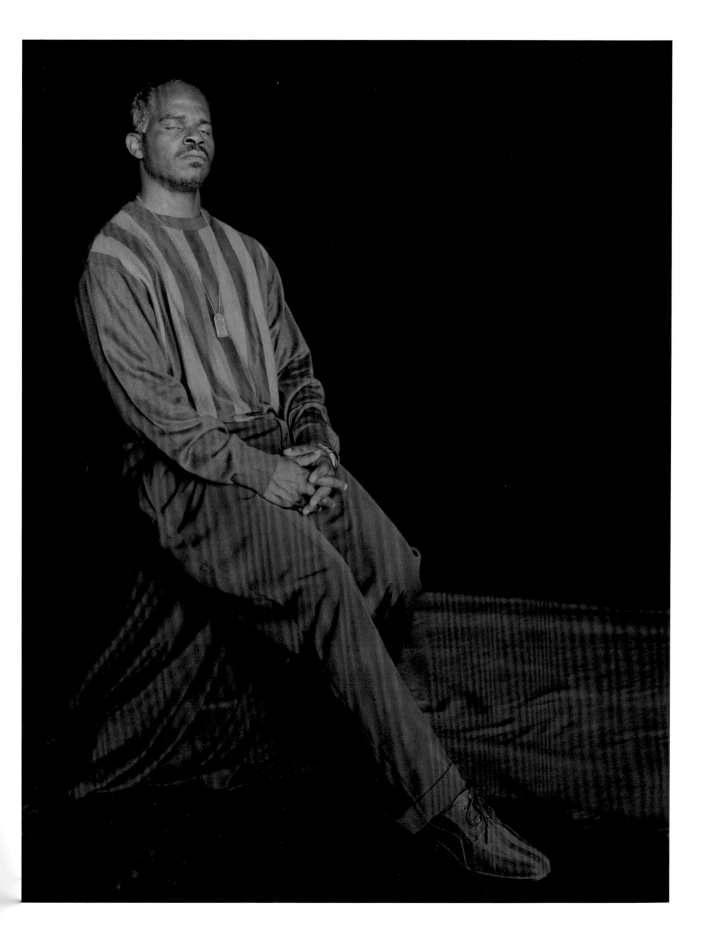

*Flees the Khmer Rouge*

In September *1994, Nary Na, a petite fourteen-year-old Cambodian girl, was found brutally murdered behind the Casa Linda shopping center in East Dallas. Death was the result of multiple blunt force injuries and a wire coat hanger twisted around her neck. Police immediately questioned Entre Nax Karage, who was engaged to the young woman according to Cambodian customs. The police claimed he killed the girl in a jealous rage. In fact, he had spent the afternoon looking for Nary after she failed to return with his car and even stopped a police cruiser to report her missing. The police immediately focused on him, going with the theory that the boyfriend is always the main suspect in a woman's death. Karage gave the police a written statement insisting on his innocence, allowed them to search his car, and passed a polygraph. Because there was no physical evidence linking him to the murder, Karage's attorney asked for a nonjury trial before a judge. The prosecution insisted that Karage had a motive—jealousy—but did not present any forensic evidence, even though semen and blood were recovered from the crime scene. Tests showed that the victim had sexual intercourse shortly before she was killed, but the prosecution's theory was that it had been consental. A language barrier also hindered his defense.*

# Entre Nax Karage

**INCIDENT DATE:** September 1994

**WRONGFUL CONVICTION:** Murder

**AGE ENTERING PRISON:** 27

**AGE LEAVING PRISON:** 34

**WRONGFUL TIME SERVED:** 7 years

*Convicted and sentenced to life*

*Becomes healer and wise man of Coffield Prison*

*Exonerated*

1997    2004 2006

# Dreams

Karage was only eight years old when the Khmer Rouge executed his father, a Cambodian monk. He and his mother fled to the United States to escape the "killing fields." His defense witnesses, members of Dallas's Cambodian community, had to speak through an interpreter at the trial. Despite their testimony in broken English that he was with them at the time of the murder, Karage was convicted by the judge and sentenced to life in prison. Repeated appeals from his attorneys for DNA testing were all denied by the judge and the district attorney as "too costly and a waste of time." He remained in prison for seven more years.

During that time, he gained a reputation among his fellow inmates as a healer, or shaman, following in the footsteps of his great-grandmother, a noted healer in their native Cambodia. He also says that while in prison he was regularly visited by his ancestors during his dreams. They taught him ancient wisdom and revealed to him in a vision that "Good will be repaid with good, and evil with evil."

In 2003, the court granted his request to run the DNA from the victim's body against a database of convicted sex offenders. It came back with a match: Keith Jordan, a black man who lived near the Casa Linda shopping center. He was already in jail for aggravated kidnapping and sexual assault of another fourteen-year-old girl. In a rather cruel twist of fate, Jordan was tried for that sexual assault in the same courthouse on the same day Karage was found guilty of murdering Nary Na. Presented with this new evidence, Governor Rick Perry granted Karage a full pardon.

Because imagery and visions played such a role in Entre's journey, the language of poetry best portrays the dreams that sustained him during his wait for justice, so I have written his story as a poem.

One of the paintings Entre made in prison with dye from the colored shells of M&M's he purchased from the commissary.

# Entre Nax Karage

*Leaving Cambodia,*
*a father, dumped into a mass grave*
*still breathing. Those in the hospital*
*who couldn't walk, were thrown*
*into a pit.*
*A family, escaping through rice fields,*
*mother, brother, sister, grandmother.*
*A child, so hungry he grabbed*
*a crab, glowing red against the sharp green*
*of the earth*
*and bit into it alive.*

*Coming to America*
*they had never seen a car*
*go in reverse.*

*The son*
*changed his name,*
*becoming*
*Entre Nax Karage: A Dragon-like Eagle who Lives in the Clouds.*
*This son, in dreams*
*saw who he was and where he came from,*
*but he didn't listen or care to understand.*
*His teacher, this tall*
*and white-robed ancestor, was left*
*to disappear into the room's*
*dark corners.*

The bride, Nary Na,
was fourteen and beautiful,
dark eyes set wide.
In the drainage ditch, her shirt
was left loose around her neck,
soaked with what a hammer does
to your skull.

We pay for the sins of our fathers and mothers,
the sins of our past lives, ourselves.

Entre cannot skin and debone
a fish, he stops to pray for a snake
who has been hit in the street.
"Someone you love,
you wouldn't let an ant
crawl on her," not an ant.

In prison
he scraped colors
from magazines and
M&M shells, when he didn't have money
to buy paint.
Art and visions were blurred
with orange. Purples and blues
bled into dreams.
He was taken to Royal Temples
and deep-forested places with no bars.
He began to understand where he came from,
he began to understand who he was.

*This man fell to his knees*
*in moments of grief and doubt.*
*But the good spirits of*
*bad men*
*would comfort him and give thanks,*
*because he*
*brought calm into a world*
*where only chaos is born.*

*In dreams*
*his head was cut off,*
*but out of the soft-flowing blood,*
*another would grow in its place.*

*We will all be reborn.*

Religious articles from
Entre's home shrine.

"Good will be repaid with good,

and evil with evil."

In 1997, *Christopher Scott was arrested on a charge of capital murder. He was wrongfully convicted of the crime and spent more than twelve years behind bars in the Texas Department of Criminal Justice's Correctional Institutions Division Unit in Huntsville. He was released only after Alonzo Hardy, who was convicted of another crime in 2009, made a prison confession that he and another man had actually committed the robbery and murder. The case, which prosecutor Mike Ware said boiled down to mistaken eyewitness testimony, is a rare exoneration because it* did not *include DNA evidence. Scott was freed on October 23, 2009.*

# Christopher Scott

**INCIDENT DATE:** April 7, 1997

**WRONGFUL CONVICTION:** Capital murder

**AGE ENTERING PRISON:** 27

**AGE LEAVING PRISON:** 39

**WRONGFUL TIME SERVED:** 12 years

*Convicted and sentenced to life*

*Brandi stops visiting*

*Exonerated and sees Brandi at his release*

1997

2009

# Love

Christopher Scott is not angry.

Christopher Scott is in love.

Oddly enough, his narrative is not so much a prison tale as a love story. Christopher learned the hard way what the Apostle Paul meant in his letter to the Corinthians when he wrote, "Love is patient."

Christopher's legal struggles began on April 27, 1997, when Alfonzo Aguilar was murdered in front of his wife during a home-invasion robbery. Christopher and his friend Claude Simmons were whisked off to jail despite the fact that neither of them matched the shooter's description, neither had any gunshot residue on him, and no physical evidence linked them to the murder.

The police brought the widow, Celia Escobedo, into the room where Christopher was sitting and asked if he was the shooter. After she identified him, he was charged with capital murder. There was such a lack of evidence against him that prosecutors went through three jury panels until they finally found twelve people who said they could consider sentencing a man to life in prison without any physical evidence. And they did: Christopher was found guilty and given a life sentence. He spent the next twelve years sitting in a Texas prison for a murder he did not commit.

Christopher's response to this institutionalized whirlwind of a wrongful conviction seems strangely peaceful now. He says that when he went to prison he only weighed about 130 pounds, but now, after thirteen years, he's 220. It is a strong 220 but one that looks as if you laid your head on his chest, it would feel like a rock but more like the earth. Prison forced him to change. He had to get strong to stay alive and to protect what he believed was his.

And what he believed was his was Brandi Simmons.

His love story started the day he saw an attractive seventeen-year-old cashier at Tom Thumb. He talks about the first time he saw her, "the new girl up at the front." Brandi was gorgeous, but all he could see was her smile.

She noticed him too. She liked to watch him work, lifting boxes in the produce section. She liked him, but she made him wait. They were friends for a long time before they became lovers. At the time, he could never imagine the years of waiting that lay ahead. He only knew that he loved her. Soon, "We were always together. When she walk, I walk. When she ride, I ride. When she go to bed, I go to bed. You know, that's just how it was. We were together seven days a week. We was committed. We was living together. We was already planning a future." When Christopher left the house they shared on the night he was arrested, all their plans were put on indefinite hold.

Once in prison, it was hard to be apart. Even her visits were difficult. "You know our emotion and feeling was so strong for each other. We'd be feeling it through the glass."

The separation was practically unbearable. It made Christopher feel lonely, particularly during the holidays. "Like, man, I could be OK through the whole year, but them holidays. Then I'd remember the last Christmas I had with Brandi. We were in our house together, we had our own place, and we did it all ourselves. We even decorated our own tree. In prison, that would be the time that I hate. I know it's supposed to be a joyous occasion, but during that time I really got sad, and I thought about it more than I should."

Even when he felt sad, Christopher always believed she would be waiting for him when he got out. That belief seemed to be the one thing that kept him going. He grabbed that thought tightly and held onto it.

"I had a lot of faith in Brandi. She motivates me, she keeps me going. She gives me that drive, that push. When I look in the mirror, I want to see the reflection of her in me. And when she looks in the mirror, I want her to see something of me that's in her. With us it's always been like that."

Christopher realized pretty quickly that the only way to survive in prison would be to spend every minute of every day trying to stay out of trouble. To him, that meant striving to be a reflection of the goodness in Brandi. He was incarcerated at the Coffield Unit where the majority of his cellblock was gang affiliated. That made staying out of trouble a full-time occupation. Another issue he had to deal with was avoiding guards and officers who looked for any excuse to write prisoners up.

"If you brushed a guy's arm in line," he recalls, "that could be interpreted as a sexual advance case."

Somehow Christopher managed to keep his nose clean. He got into trouble for smoking a cigarette during his first week but hasn't smoked another one since. You wonder why he spent every second of every day staying out of trouble. It wasn't as if he was going to earn any time off for good behavior, especially while serving a life sentence with seemingly no chance of parole. Hoping for some encouragement, he showed his case to a fellow prisoner.

"A white guy; he was a prison lawyer. And he say, 'Man, it's no way you're going to beat this case.' I'm like 'Why you say that?' And he's like, 'You don't have no DNA in this case. A case has never been won nowhere, ever, without DNA. The only way it will happen is if the guy who really did this confesses, and that's not going to happen.'"

When asked how he kept on believing against such long odds, Christopher replies, "He kind of crushed me a little bit, but I never gave up faith. I kept believing somehow I would get back to her because we had such a good life together, and I didn't want to give up hope."

He never doubted he would be found innocent. As you listen to him, it sounds as if he was living in some sort of fantasy world. You want to shake him out of his delusional state and shout, "Weren't you furious every day? Aren't you angry about the years they took from you?" One can't argue with his logic because somehow his dream came true.

However, Christopher and Brandi's love story is far from perfect. After he was incarcerated, he began to feel guilty that Brandi was holding onto their relationship when he could not be there for her.

One of the things he cherished most was a letter from her in which she wrote of how she always felt loved and protected with him. Reading her swirling, cursive handwriting over and over again made him

Brandi visiting Christopher in prison.

realize that he was in the one place where he could not protect her or even be there for her. It took a toll on him. Knowing all the while that he would never stop loving her, he realized that for her sake he had to let her go.

"It eats you up mentally. So it finally got to the point where I'd rather for her just to go on her way."

When Christopher told Brandi she should move on, she got angry and questioned if he truly loved her, but now she realizes it was the hardest thing he ever did. For a while, she refused to cut him loose. She kept visiting, and waited for three more years until at last she realized he was right—she had to move on.

A letter and a picture from Brandi.

He remembers the exact moment he knew Brandi had made her decision. On a routine trip to the commissary to buy a toothbrush and toothpaste, he was told by a guard he would have to come back the next day because there was a hold on his account. When he asked what that meant, the guard responded it usually meant there was an unusually large amount of money in the account.

Christopher walked back to his cell, confused. He slumped down on his bunk and wondered who could have made such a large deposit. After a few minutes, he realized it was Brandi. The $2,500 in his account was her good-bye. The money lasted him for the rest of his stay in Coffield, but he didn't see Brandi again during the next seven years. Even though he knew she was gone, he held onto her as his reason to continue. It didn't seem to faze him that now it was a one-way love affair.

 "So that's how it was," he says. "It's like when she left me, the love got stronger."

He knew he still had to be able to look into the mirror and find her goodness within him or he would break down in the darkness of Texas prison life. He would trudge through mind-numbing days waiting for the evening when he could be in his cell and look at his pictures of Brandi.

"I used to look at the old pictures that I had to try to get me through the day or whatever. That helped out a whole lot, going through the old pictures, just wishing I was there and praying that one day I'd be back in that position again."

Other nights he would search the dial on the small transistor radio purchased with some of Brandi's good-bye money, hoping to hear their favorite song, "Who Can I Run To?" by Xscape. He somehow felt closer to her when he heard the song's final line, "All it takes is time and patience to bring you near."

While the days remain the same in prison, life goes on in the outside world. Eventually he heard through the prison grapevine that Brandi had a baby. He had mixed emotions about this news, a combination of intense sadness, torment, and wistful happiness—sadness because he had always wanted a daughter; torment because he thought that if he hadn't been wrongfully convicted, the baby could have been his child; happiness because in spite of how much it hurt him, he wanted good things for Brandi. He tried to be happy by telling himself, "A baby is a good thing, a beautiful thing."

When Christopher could put aside his jealousy, he was strangely pleased because he knew that if Brandi was happy, everything was going to be all right.

He soon lost even that cold comfort when worse news arrived.

People began telling him that although Brandi was still with the baby's father, the relationship had soured, and she was in a very rough situation. Even this news, which would drive most people into a blind rage or a deep depression, perversely kept him looking ahead, taking it one day at a time. He knew that if he continued to stay out of trouble, he would eventually be released and finally be able to protect her.

Anyone who has ever gone through a long separation from a loved one dreams of the day they will be reunited. Every prisoner dreams of the day he will be set free. In Christopher Scott's dream, these were one and the same day. He prayed that when he walked into the courtroom, Brandi would be there, but he knew that dream had little chance of coming true. By the time he learned he was going to be exonerated, he had neither seen nor heard from her in more than seven years. He knew he couldn't write or call her because he knew she was in a difficult situation with her boyfriend. Refusing to give up hope, he wrote a letter to her aunt with a small note folded inside for Brandi, telling her his court date.

The scene in the Dallas courtroom where Christopher's exoneration hearing was held was overwhelming. More than two hundred people were jammed inside, and about two hundred more were waiting out in the hallway. As he walked through the doors, the first face he saw was his mother's, but tempering his excitement and joy was the disappointment of not seeing Brandi. After he was released, he was hugged and squeezed from every direction by loving family members and friends. He shot a glance through the crowd, and at last he saw Brandi standing alone in the corner. Smiling.

Today, after six months of freedom, there is an air of shyness between Christopher and Brandi. They giggle as they describe buying a new copy of the old Xscape CD they loved before Christopher went away. Now they can listen to their favorite song together again. It seems strange for two people who longed for each other for so many years to appear so tentative and disconnected, but a twelve-year separation takes its toll on a relationship. They have changed from love-struck teenagers to life-hardened adults. Brandi has a child and the emotional scars from a deeply wounding relationship. Christopher has lived through the pain of a wrongful conviction and the horror of twelve hard years inside a Texas prison.

Their lives ahead will be difficult, and their future is far from certain. Somehow they must make up for more than a decade of stolen time.

They will have to relearn their love.

On May 7, 1985, *a brutal rape and home invasion robbery took place in the Dallas suburb of Richardson. Two weeks later, the nineteen-year-old female victim picked Thomas McGowan out of a seven-person photo lineup. Ironically, although she pointed to the picture of McGowan, a picture of her real rapist was looking up at her from another photograph in the lineup. Nearly twenty-three years later, DNA testing proved that man to be the actual attacker. Once the victim identified McGowan, things looked bad for the twenty-six-year-old who was living in Richardson. He drove a car similar to the one driven by the rapist, had no solid alibi, and had previously been convicted of burglary. Jurors believed the victim, and sentenced him to two life sentences, which the judge ordered to be served consecutively. McGowan spent twenty-three years in the TDCJ's Ferguson Unit until DNA testing freed him in 2008. The real attacker has since been located in a Texas prison, where he is serving time for bank robbery, but was not tried for this rape because the statute of limitations had expired.*

# Thomas McGowan

| | |
|---:|:---|
| **INCIDENT DATE:** | May 7, 1985 |
| **WRONGFUL CONVICTION:** | Burglary of a habitation and aggravated sexual assault |
| **AGE ENTERING PRISON:** | 26 |
| **AGE LEAVING PRISON:** | 49 |
| **WRONGFUL TIME SERVED:** | 23 years |

# Adaptation

At age twenty-six, the last thing Thomas McGowan thought he might become was a slave. Maybe a student, a husband, or a father but never a slave. Arrested and convicted of burglary and sexual assault with a deadly weapon, Thomas was sentenced to two consecutive life sentences. He remembers thinking he was in trouble when he walked into the courtroom and saw "one of those Republican lady judges."

He also speaks of Dallas.

Coming from the smaller Texas town of Wichita Falls, he expected Dallas to be "the city," and it was, with its bright lights and tall buildings. But after Thomas was arrested and sat through his trial, he says he began to see that there was still a lot of "country" in this "city," and it didn't take much for a black man to be sent to prison at the drop of a hat.

But Thomas didn't really learn about "country" until he arrived at the Ferguson Unit in Midway, Texas. He remembers the day he was shipped off from Dallas. The guards came to his cell in the county jail dragging a long chain with handcuffs as they marched down the cellblock. The sound of the metal flying through the air and landing on the concrete floor with an earth-shattering clank is one that he will never forget. Chained to twenty other men, Thomas rode the bus for two hours to the Ferguson Unit, watching the highways and the cars as he moved farther and farther from freedom until "all you could see was forest"—miles and miles of pine trees with timber trucks roaring and rushing by. This journey, his "middle passage," soon came to an end when he stepped off the bus and saw the horses.

He had now entered what to him was a "whole 'nother world—straight up country." All he could see and taste and smell was dust.

"As soon as I got off the bus, I'm looking and I'm thinking here is a guy with a shotgun in the back and another two guys with guns up front. I remember I used to watch movies and see stuff like this, and now here I am going through it. This whole scene is messed up."

The guards were "good old boys," with the clinking of their spurs preceding them as they walked down the block. At intake, Thomas was classified by age and offense, assigned a unit, and then given his number, #417200. The walk from intake to his cell was like going through a tunnel, a tunnel of dust, brick, stone, and barbed wire fences that seemed to have no light at the end. The first night in his cell he heard a seventeen- or eighteen-year-old kid next to him talking about shooting and paralyzing a young girl.

"He was just a kid, but he was a killer."

Thomas didn't belong here. His cell was nine-by-five feet with bars covered in chipped green paint, a sink, a toilet, a board on the wall for a shelf, and a steel bunk. When the cell doors rolled shut, a wave of panic washed over him.

"I'm closed up; I can't get out."

That night in prison, Thomas learned he was claustrophobic.

It took him until three in the morning to get the guards to bring him a mattress. For the first part of the night he lay curled up on the cold, green-painted steel platform, waiting. Waiting for his mattress, waiting for the morning, waiting for someone to realize that he was not supposed to be here. But no one did, so Thomas did the only thing he could.

"I put it in my mind that I just got to go on with it no matter how I'm feeling. I can't do anything about it. The only thing in my mind is that I got to keep looking at the steps I'm going through and the steps ahead of me."

Only a few hours later, Thomas found out there were things he had to adjust to he had never imagined. At four in the morning, the cell doors rolled open. An exhausted Thomas watched them open, heard the commotion, and remained lying in bed.

"McGowan," boomed a voice. "Why the hell aren't you at work?"

No one had told him what to do or where to go.

"Shut up; just be at work tomorrow morning."

When the doors opened the next morning, he was up. He was given a white pair of pants, a shirt, and a pair of black work boots. He put them on and got on the bus. All he saw in every direction was cotton, rows and rows of cotton. After he got off the bus, a field boss sitting on a horse with a gun hollered, "Catch a row," and #417200 was handed a long, dirty, nasty brown burlap sack.

Thomas remembers being in shock and thinking, "I will never pick cotton. I will never be a slave," but after a moment's hesitation, two guards towering over him on horseback herded him to a row.

A book that strengthened Thomas in prison.

At seven o'clock in the morning, the cotton was still wet with dew and sticky to the touch, but as the day wore on, Thomas began to miss the early morning coolness because Midway, Texas, on a July afternoon is hotter than hell. As he worked, Thomas said to himself, "Man, I cannot believe this; I'm picking cotton. I've become a slave."

Thomas hated it and hated what he had become, but in time, he picked too many rows of cotton to count. He soon fell into a regular routine of working for a few months and then deciding he'd had enough.

"One day I just said I quit. It was too hot."

The days he refused to work he was sent to solitary where the walls rattled with unbearable noise. The foreign trill of Hispanic gang members conversing and the screams of the mentally ill inmates made it seem that solitary was not the most suitable name for this Tower of Babel. This cycle of working, then refusing meant Thomas didn't move out of the fields for fifteen years. He says that in order to survive, you have to adjust.

"That's when I made up my mind that I've got to adjust so I can have some kind of freedom.

"I didn't want to be staying there locked up in the cells all the time and stuff like this. It goes back to what we said: adjustment, you have to adjust. I wasn't going to conform—I was going to adjust."

Thomas watched and learned.

"I'd see the other guys doing it like exercise and I'd say, 'Well, OK then, I'm going to go on and do it like it's exercise.'" He began to see the fieldwork as a competition.

"That's the only way I could adjust to it. Instead of thinking 'Man, I'm innocent; this is slave work,' and starting to buck it, I just started to look at it as a physical activity."

Some days, the field bosses added an incentive, telling the men that the team that finished first would move to the front of the line in the dining hall.

"We used to love it when they made fried chicken, because you could smell it cooking all morning. The first crew to finish in the field got to eat first."

He also began to cherish his time in the rec room, working out on the equipment and playing basketball. He began to follow sports, creating a reason to go to the dayroom and watch a Dallas Cowboys game or the world boxing championship. Boxing was his favorite. He loved that moment when the victorious boxer lifted his arms above his head in celebration.

Despite being wrongfully convicted and hating the backbreaking fieldwork, Thomas McGowan began to adapt. Eventually this new mentality allowed him to move out of the fields and into a job doing janitorial work. As time passed, he began to notice other men's numbers—#632900, #718400. Thomas, #417200, was getting older. Younger inmates started calling him "School," short for "old school," a title reserved for inmates who had been in prison a long time.

"These people down here, they'll hide you, man. They'll give you so much time it will just hide you from the world, and you won't never come back."

He began to fear that he would die in prison, or worse, that his mother might die, never knowing for certain that her son was innocent. He prayed every night that neither of those things would happen. One day his prayers were answered.

On June 11, 2008, Thomas McGowan became #16: the sixteenth man in Dallas County to be exonerated by DNA evidence. The #16 is one he is proud to carry because it is not the number of a slave or a prisoner but a number that symbolizes justice.

Thomas stands about five feet, nine inches and is a fairly thin man. He is not a boxer, but on the day he walked out of the courtroom a free man, the Innocence Project's Jason Craig and Barry Scheck stood on either side of him and held up his arms. Like a boxer, he had championed his cause. At last he felt victorious.

"Yeah, I'm the champ. I came out victorious. Through everything, you know, no matter what, God brings you through it. If He chooses you, He brings you through it."

Despite Thomas's release, life on the outside hasn't been easy. His relationship with his mother is strained. After twenty-three years of praying to be with her, he says they really have little in common.

"Things change. You know, I think the hardest part is my mother. After being away from her so long, I couldn't believe I'd be sitting in a room with her. Now we are in the room together, but we can't hardly talk because so much has gone."

They often sit in a room together, unsure of what to say.

He also mourns the fact that he cannot be a father. "I've never even had the chance to see a child grow up. I think that would be a wonderful thing."

Today Thomas McGowan is not a slave, but he also is not a father nor a husband. No one can replace what he has lost.

"Yeah, I'm the champ. I came out victorious.
Through everything, you know, no matter what,
God brings you through it. If He chooses you,
He brings you through it."

Voted best dressed all four
years of high school

Convicted and
sentenced to 2 life sentences
plus 20 years

1985

When a *female cashier at a Waxahachie, Texas, convenience store was raped during a robbery, police picked up Victor Thomas for questioning and soon focused on him as their prime suspect. Based almost entirely upon the victim's eyewitness testimony, Thomas was convicted and sentenced to 2 life sentences plus 20 years for kidnapping. On April 17, 2002, more than fifteen years later, he was freed from prison after DNA testing proved he was not the rapist.*

# Victor Thomas

| | |
|---:|:---|
| **INCIDENT DATE:** | October 24, 1985 |
| **WRONGFUL CONVICTION:** | Rape, kidnapping, and robbery |
| **AGE ENTERING PRISON:** | 26 |
| **AGE LEAVING PRISON:** | 41 |
| **WRONGFUL TIME SERVED:** | 15 years, 7 months, 6 days |

# Work

"God will provide for you, but you've got to go get it. You've got to sweat."

Victor Thomas has been sweating his entire life. Growing up in a family of fifteen children, he saw his father work hard to provide for them. His father was fifty years old when Victor was born, but he continued laboring well past retirement age to support his family. When he was about five years old, Victor blinded himself in one eye with an antenna, but his partial lack of sight did not stop him from playing sports or holding down a job. Victor worked in the "real world," earning enough money to buy fancy clothes and be voted best dressed all four years of high school. He also made time to work at home. Victor was given the responsibility of serving as the family chef. When he describes his favorite recipe for cornbread, you can almost taste its richness and feel it crumbling softly in your fingers.

After graduating high school, Victor attended Bishop College for a year, but when his family's house burned down around Christmas, he came home and started working full time to help out.

That's when things took a turn for the worse.

His family was in shambles, his girlfriend was pregnant, and a few months later, he was arrested and sent to prison for robbery. He was able to attend college during his three-year prison term. He took some basic classes, like U.S. history and English, but more importantly, he studied the culinary arts.

He was eventually released from prison, and the moment the bus pulled into Dallas, Victor stepped off and got a job. He saw some men sweating in the street, digging holes for telephone poles. They handed him a jackhammer, and he put in twelve hours of hard labor before he went home to see his girlfriend and daughter.

When Victor got out of prison the first time, he wanted his cake and ice cream "and to eat it too," but "you've got to work," he says. "You've got to work."

For a while, things went well. Victor was working hard and putting food on the table. He got married and his wife became pregnant again, this time with a boy. However, things were not as they appeared. Victor discovered that his wife was seeing another man and was uncertain if her unborn child was even his. So Victor did what any smart man would do in his situation—he went to talk to his mom.

His mother divorced Victor's father right after the last of their fifteen children left the house and was now living in Waxahachie. "She waited until the last one was grown, then she left his butt."

Still, he wanted her advice, so Victor and his brother drove down at the beginning of November. True to form, after being at his mom's house for about twenty minutes, he went out and got a job at a local construction site. He was working there for a week or two, trying to figure out his life, when the police arrested him at a local bar after he finished work.

If what he has pieced together is accurate, the chain of events that led to his conviction mirrored the novel *To Kill a Mockingbird*. Victor describes a small-town scandal that involved the white newspaper owner's daughter and the racially charged cover-up that ensued. While in the county jail, Victor wrote a ten-page letter to the girl's father, hoping to appeal to his sense of decency, but he never got a response. The girl appeared in court to identify Victor, but she never met his gaze and left the courtroom before the verdict was read.

"The all-white jury went to Underwood's Barbeque for lunch," he recalls ruefully. "They came back into the courtroom with toothpicks still in their mouths, and within five minutes, I had two lifes and twenty years."

Once Victor arrived at the Coffield Unit, he already knew what he had to do: put his head down and get to work.

"If you don't apply yourself, what are you going to turn into out in the real world?" he asks. "You're going to get institutionalized. No one is going to help you. You have to do it yourself, motivate yourself. You have to rehabilitate yourself. Innocent or guilty, you have to say, 'Life goes on and I'm gonna be a productive person in this world, even though I'm locked up.' You don't have to work, and you ain't gonna get paid—not in Texas. In other words, if you can work in prison, you can work out in the world."

For three years, Victor worked in the fields. Because he had worked all of his life and done fieldwork as a child, he made a good hand. He quickly gained the respect of the field bosses, which wasn't an easy thing to do. Whenever the bosses cashed their paychecks, they would come out into the fields with a huge roll of bills, spread it out in their fingers for all the inmates to see, and say, "I think I'll use this to take your mom out tonight" or "Maybe your sister needs a new, cute little outfit."

Unlike the other inmates, Victor didn't take the bait and soon moved to a better job. He no longer picked cotton. Instead he sat up in the truck and poured in the cotton the other prisoners brought to him.

On days when the work was slow, he was assigned by Officer MacDougal, a field boss who particularly liked Victor, to search for arrowheads. Victor's prison nickname was "One Eye" because he is partially blind, but ironically he's one of those people who can find things.

"I'm real good. Like say one of y'all lose an earring. I could find it."

While other prisoners might find one arrowhead after several days of looking, he could find two or three a day. Arrowheads brought a good price. Pretty soon, Officer MacDougal, whose pockets were a bit heavier due to Victor's arrowhead-hunting ability, put in a good word for him. Victor was assigned to the kitchen, just as he had requested.

Once Victor got into the kitchen, he almost felt like he was back home.

"You didn't have to go out in the fields and be all hot. You could just go in the freezers, cool off, stand around, and eat up everything. You can have fun in there. It's an enjoyment. It wasn't even a job to me. Whenever I got into the kitchen, I got full."

His timing could not have been better. Victor showed up in the kitchen just as the head cook was completing his sentence. He showed Victor the ropes and then left the position available for him to fill. Victor soon became the kitchen system's troubleshooter, a big responsibility when you're feeding three thousand inmates three meals a day.

"You got a hundred-gallon pot, stainless steel. How you gonna cook without overcooking three bags of rice? I'm talking the fifty-pound bags. You got to cook for about three thousand people, three meals a day."

Although he didn't have to, he volunteered for extra shifts in the kitchen. Victor often worked up to sixteen hours a day, especially whenever they cooked fried chicken, everyone's favorite.

Victor also combated the burden of wrongful imprisonment with his comedic talents. "I don't like being sad, so I tell jokes. In prison, I didn't ever listen to music because it made me sad. Holidays were particularly bad, but being in the kitchen helped. Like on my birthday I could make myself a cake."

What really seemed to get Victor through his sentence was work, but after a while "just work didn't seem to be working." Throughout his years in prison, Victor's mother would write to him and always ask the same thing, "Why don't you try Jesus?"

"I told her I didn't believe all that Jesus crap stuff. I didn't. I wasn't even trying to."

Nearly a decade passed, and with each letter, her handwriting got bigger and sloppier until one day he realized she probably didn't have much longer. So Victor finally decided to put more effort into his faith before it was too late. He worked on giving God the glory, he worked on saying "Hallelujah" and meaning it, and he worked on his ability to forgive.

"I was supposed to rot in prison, but instead I learned glory."

The first person that Victor had to forgive was, surprisingly, God.

"I was angry at God. I had cursed Him and everything."

He then slowly and systematically began a trail of forgiveness that covered his lifetime. He forgave his mother for divorcing his father; he forgave his own wife for divorcing him; he forgave the girl who falsely accused him of rape; he forgave the jury who ate at Underwood's Barbeque; and he even forgave the judge who sentenced him.

"I had said if I ever get out, I'm going to dig his grave up, and put a chain on him, and run down the street 'til he disintegrate. I said I was going to get him. I told God this."

Now, Victor began to pray for him.

With this forgiveness came change. Soon the ball began to roll toward Victor's exoneration through DNA testing. Whenever he describes getting freed, he says, "I'm not lucky, I'm blessed, but I didn't get out easy; I gave it to God."

It seems, His way worked.

The day Victor was released from prison, he went out and did what he had always done—he got a job.

His brother owned a company that installed appliances in fast-food chains and Victor started working for him. After he received his compensation from the State of Texas, he decided to open up a restaurant himself, but those dreams were derailed by a bad relationship.

"All that time, who was I thinking about being with? I had nobody. I was abandoned and hurt. The ladies in the magazines, they were my friends."

Fifteen years in prison often leads to quick decisions, and a freshly stocked bank account can attract questionable young women. It didn't take long until those two met up with each other. After Victor was taken for all he was worth, he left Dallas.

"I cried all the way down I-20 until I ended up in Tyler."

Back in the piney woods of East Texas, Victor started rebuilding his life. He met a good woman, Carolyne, and they've been dating for the last five years. They're thinking of buying a house and getting married, but he wants it to be right this time.

"Carolyne isn't the kind that wants my money. You can tell when a lady just want to mess over you, because we've all been through it."

He still works, traveling to local schools and churches to speak about his experience. "It's the good times now. We already suffered. Let go and live the good life."

"God will provide for you, but you've got
to go get it. You've got to sweat."

On February *18, 1984, a woman awakened in her Dallas County home to discover a man in her bedroom. After raping her, he locked her in a closet and left. Although the attacker wore a mask, the victim identified then-seventeen-year-old Eugene Henton as her assailant. On the advice of his attorney, he accepted a plea bargain, was found guilty, and was sentenced to four years in prison. Paroled after eighteen months but unable to find employment because of his criminal past as a sex offender, he turned to selling drugs. Arrested and convicted on drug charges, he was returned to prison with a sixty-two-year enhanced sentence, the result of being a sex offender arrested while on parole. With help from the Dallas County public defender's office, he applied for DNA testing on the 1984 rape conviction. The tests proved that another man was the rapist and Henton's conviction was overturned, but he remained in prison on the drug charges. In 2007, all drug charges were reduced to time served. He was released from prison on October 26, 2007.*

# Eugene Henton

**INCIDENT DATE:** February 18, 1984

**WRONGFUL CONVICTION:** Sexual assault

**AGE ENTERING PRISON:** 18

**AGE LEAVING PRISON:** 20

**WRONGFUL TIME SERVED:** 18 months

*Returned to prison
on drug charges enhanced
by wrongful conviction*　　　*Learns Arabic*　　　　　　　*Exonerated*

1993　　　　　　　　　　　　　　　　　　　2007

# Words

Eugene Henton is a big man.

His calm demeanor and smooth diction offer no clues to his past. Soft-spoken, articulate, and overly polite in a six-foot, two-inch frame, Eugene is like a UN diplomat, fluent in Arabic and Spanish, in an NFL lineman's body. When he opens his mouth, you immediately recognize that there is more to this imposing character than meets the eye.

During his childhood in Tallulah, Louisiana, many of Eugene's uncles did "hard time" in the notorious Angola penitentiary. Because he grew up in a family of fighters, he learned how to fight at an early age, but today, he faces a different opponent. He's struggling to vanquish a shadow that follows him whenever he ventures out into the real world.

"There are no psychiatrists who've done twenty years in prison for a crime they did not commit, so they really couldn't offer me a solution. It's normal to hold people at a distance, even going into the grocery store," he says. "The stigma still haunts you."

That "stigma" is time in a Texas prison for a rape he did not commit. The day he met his court-appointed attorney, he was told, "Son, you have two problems here. You're poor and you're black. You cannot fight this."

Advised by his lawyer to accept a plea bargain of four years, he pled guilty, hoping he would be able to get out in two. Going in at seventeen, a lanky six-foot-two, and weighing only 160 pounds, he knew that to survive he was going to have to look, talk, and be tough.

You can't enter a federal penitentiary until you turn eighteen, so Eugene and two other kids were held in a special unit until they were old enough to go to hell.

Handcuffed together, they stepped off the bus at the Ferguson Unit. Immediately Eugene knew that every single person around them was already sizing them up; predators lined the walls waiting and watching, trying to assess who looked weak and who looked like he would put up a fight.

"They are looking at your posture, your demeanor, your walk, everything."

Eugene knew he had to be a fighter.

In 1984, Texas prisons used the Building Tenders program, or BT, which meant that the inmates ran the prisons. Selected prisoners moved up to the status of trusty and served as guards. The way Eugene tells it, the BTs ran everything, knew everything, and worse, were in control.

"Those inmates had the power to do what they wanted. If they wanted to rape a guy, they would get the real guards to open his cell, then the trusty inmates would go in there and do whatever. That's how it was in '84 when I arrived."

On his second day, one of the BTs came to his cell, looked down at the recently issued prison work boots on Eugene's feet, and asked, "What size shoes are those?"

In that moment, Eugene knew this was a test. If he handed over his shoes, he would be pegged as a weakling, someone to be taken advantage of, used, or manipulated.

"So I got this smirky smile on my face that I always put on when I'm ready to fight. It's this sarcastic smirk and it has a tendency to really infuriate a person. I told him, 'They're just your size.' He said, 'Take 'em off,' then I said, 'Naw, bro, if you want these, *you're* going to have to take them off.'"

The BT opened the cell door and Eugene's first prison fight was on.

It lasted only thirty seconds, but it was long enough to establish Eugene Henton as a man who wouldn't back down from a fight. When it was over, he still had his shoes. After the rumors had a few hours to spread, he had pretty much established his reputation. The other two kids that came into Ferguson with him weren't as lucky. Within a matter of weeks, they were both raped. One of them committed suicide. The other was sent to the protective custody unit for inmates in danger of repeated sexual abuse.

"My rebellion kept me strong enough to get through the experience. I wouldn't have gotten through it being passive or just conforming to the environment. I would have been victimized, taken advantage of; I was just a kid."

His troubles didn't end after that first fight, and he had plenty more to come, but he managed to be released after eighteen months, still breathing and still swinging.

Back in the real world, the language of fight he perfected in prison didn't work as well. He couldn't seem to rehabilitate.

"When I came home, I didn't want to be around my mom or my family.

"You know, they loved me, and I loved them. It's just that the hardening of that experience made me want to be alone, away from family members, and try and survive on my own."

For a while, he was homeless, spending nights in an abandoned house, showering when he could at the homes of friends and family, but the hardest part was trying to find work. On every completed job application, he was haunted by the word "rape," because the moment someone sees that word in hard, black letters, everything changes.

Some people scooted their chairs back in horror, others let their mouths drop wide open, and women, especially, shot him a look of terror mixed with disgust. After only a few job interviews, he couldn't take it anymore. He entered a profession that didn't require an application or a background check. One where "they didn't care one way or another whether I had gone to prison or not."

Eugene started dealing drugs.

"That was the worst choice that I could've made in my entire life was to take that way out. I should have suffered it and continued to go pick up cans or anything rather than get into the drug-selling business. It's just so much violence that's surrounding that way of living that had I had the opportunity to do it again, I would never choose that."

Unfortunately he did, and that's when things really went downhill.

In 1993, he shot a man in self-defense during a drug deal gone bad.

"I got into a fight situation. I was fighting two guys that were together. One of them hit me in the head with a bottle and I shot him.

"And that's how I get the aggravated assault case."

Eugene was tried and found guilty of assault and dealing drugs, but because of his previous rape conviction, he was given an enhanced sentence—sixty-two years—to be served in the Hughes Unit in Gatesville, Texas.

But this time around, something was different.

"I had changed. Going back that second time crushed me because now I had kids and also I was in there for something I really did do.

"Just having to come back was mentally exhausting for me. I cried. I think because of that softening I was open."

Eugene Henton's well loved Quran from his days in prison.

While awaiting transfer in the county jail, Eugene began to read the only book in his cell. It was a dictionary somebody had left behind.

"It was just a regular dictionary, and I just started looking up words and reading it. So I said to myself that I have to get something out of this, and I didn't quite know what it was that I'm looking to get, but I wanted to educate myself, I wanted to be articulate. I started a quest for knowledge."

When he entered prison for the second time, his quest continued. He took a paralegal course.

"I wanted to learn the law. This time I couldn't give up because I needed to get out and raise my kids."

One day, his new attitude allowed Eugene to see something he otherwise might have missed. He walked into the rec room and saw a man reading a bright green book with distinctive gold lettering. The book seemed to be glowing, almost pulsating as Eugene walked toward it.

"What is that?" he asked in amazement.

"It's the Quran," the inmate replied.

Then Eugene saw the writing inside the book, strange shapes and symbols sprawled across the page like nothing he had ever seen before.

"What language is that?" he asked breathlessly.

"That is Arabic," the man said. "This is the original Quran."

The man began to read the mysterious text out loud, rhythmically producing strange and beautiful sounds that Eugene never imagined the human voice could make. Questions filled Eugene's mind, but before he could ask them, the man looked at him and said, "Would you like to come with me to Taleem for evening prayers?"

They walked to the small prison chapel at dusk where thirty men were gathered. The chairs had been removed so they could lay rugs across the floor. One inmate stood at the front and introduced himself. His name was Larry Ross, but now he went by his Muslim name, Kareem. When he saw Eugene standing near the back with a few other newcomers, he announced that instead of their scheduled Arabic lessons, tonight he would review the basic principles of Islam.

As Eugene listened, all of his questions were answered. He realized instinctively that something extraordinary was happening to him.

"I felt relieved, you know? It was like my guards were down. I didn't feel that I needed to fight anymore. I felt that my fighting was done. It was emotional. It took me a lot not to cry, to bite my jaws and just to hold back the overwhelming joy that I experienced just from being there."

After the lesson, the men gathered silently in rows. They widened their stance and let their bare feet touch slightly as they knelt, bending at the waist, prostrating themselves. As they pressed their faces to the floor, each man's elbows touched those of the man beside him.

"I know this is the end of my search. It'll all catch up with me, but this is where I belong. All these different people made one solid unit, and I felt that, and I wanted to be a part of that unit, to complete that.

"So I kept coming back, and I wouldn't miss a day for years."

In the small, dirty chapel of the Hughes Unit in Gatesville, Texas, Eugene Henton finally came home.

He began to study Arabic and read the Quran for himself. Within a month, he was no longer a student but was standing at the front of the chapel, teaching lessons to his Muslim brothers. Yet despite his feelings of homecoming and welcome, there was a tension growing inside him that he could not calm.

"There are two different characters that you have," he explains. "One is that old despicable character. The other is the new character or the person that's manifested in this development.

"With these two characters, only one can exist at a time, either one or the other. The two trying to coexist together makes him hypocritical and in Arabic it's called 'Munafiq.' That's not gonna work. He will go insane. He cannot live both characters at the same time. In order for him to manifest and to be complete, one character has to go.

"So I had to slay the old character."

Eugene wrote this poem to describe his transformation:

*On a journey through the desert there are two men,*
*two characters. One is that old, despicable man,*
*Tired and haggard from years of struggle and war.*
*The other is a new man, a man with richness and wealth.*
*As they move towards the city gates,*
*bandits watch from the hills on horseback.*
*They try to decide which man to conquer, which man to kill.*
*I saw them waiting there, watching*
*and that left me a choice to make.*
*I plunged my dagger into the heart*
*of the old, miserable man and buried him*
*there in the desert. Only I know where he rests.*
*Even the bandits did not see where I took him.*
*And as the bandits came charging through the sand,*
*I reached the hill leading to the city gate.*
*Now, what if I had killed the wrong man?*
*Would they have locked their doors when they saw him*
*coming towards the walls?*
*But I made the right choice,*
*and the whole town saw him in the light*
*and met him with open arms, because*
*they knew the right one had emerged.*

After a while the men in prison begin calling Eugene by a new name, Saleem, which means safe, healthy, and secure. These are words no one would have used to describe the seventeen-year-old boy who fought so hard to survive his first stint in prison.

"I was joyous. When you become other than what you were before, you no longer act the way you used to. When you practice it every day in every situation, it becomes habituated, and then it's just natural."

He continued to read and take paralegal courses and began filing motions, writs, and affidavits. They went nowhere. One of his requests sat unanswered for thirty-one months. Finally, in 2002, he received a letter from Judge Keith Dean informing him that a DNA statute had passed and that he should file an affidavit for the evidence in his case.

Somehow authorities located the rape kit with the forensic evidence containing semen taken from the victim. Amazingly it had been preserved for more than twenty years at the Southwestern Institute for Forensic Science and was still testable. After this evidence was located, Eugene knew it was only a matter of time before the DNA tests would prove his innocence.

"It's like a ton of bricks was just lifted off my chest," recalls Eugene, "because the worst thing that could have happened was that it was destroyed."

If he could be exonerated of the rape charge, the rationale for the years added to his sentence in the assault and drug cases would be eliminated.

The results from the DNA test proved that another man had committed the rape, and Eugene had been innocent all along. On September 1, 2005, his rape conviction was overturned. In June 2007, the Texas Court of Criminal Appeals threw out his sentences in the drug and assault cases. He was finally released from prison on October 27, 2007.

By the time he walked out, he had served nearly thirteen years of his adult life in prison. One of the last inmates he saw before departing was Kareem, his Muslim leader and mentor.

"He's crying and the tears are coming down. He said, 'Saleem, I am so sorry. I've always believed you that you had a case on your back that you didn't commit. The thing that saddens me the most is that you had to stay here all these years, and I didn't know how to help you.'"

Eugene Henton emerged from prison a changed man. Today he has a commanding vocabulary and speaks three languages—English, Arabic, and Spanish. More a scholar than a fighter, it's as if he has written a eulogy for the man he used to be.

"The bad character was a product, a sum total of his bad experiences in life. That made him rigorous but callous, if you will. This person survived by all means, but there was no compassion. He was on the brink of humanity and sanity and insanity, you know? He became inhumane at times because he did not feel. No, he survived, and in order to survive he had to do things that a normal, thinking person would not do. I speak of him in the third person because he's dead; he's not here anymore. That is what I believe. And that is what made it easier for me to manifest the character that you see here now."

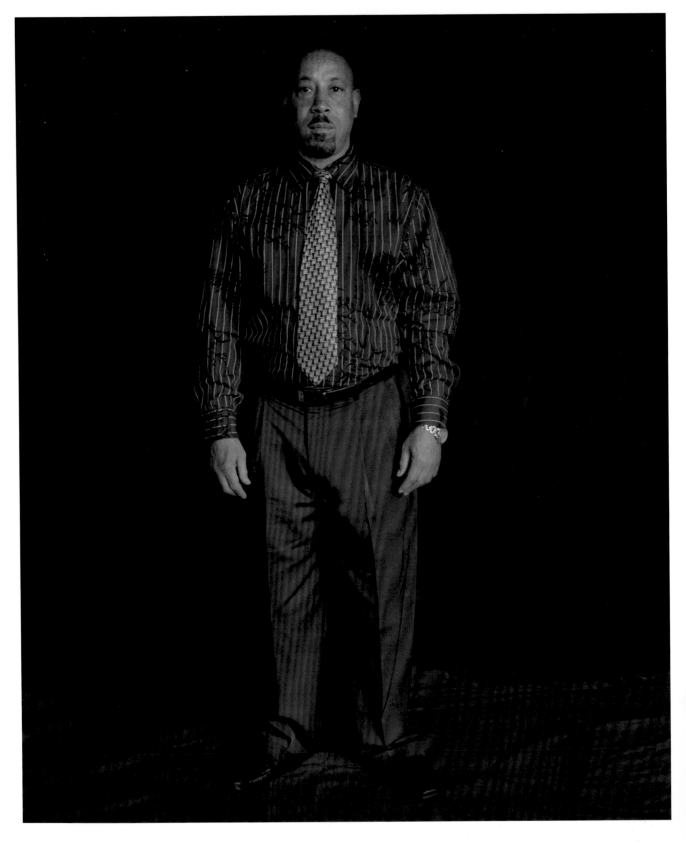

*Convicted and    Mother's    Released*
*sentenced to 20 years    death    from prison*

1983               1987

**On December** 6, 1982, a young black man raped a thirty-three-year-old woman in the laundry room of her apartment complex. Four months later, she identified Keith Turner as her assailant, based on his voice, after he walked into the break room at her job. Despite no physical evidence and defense witnesses' testimony that he was watching a football game with them at the time, Keith Turner was convicted and sentenced to twenty years. He was granted early release but spent sixteen years on parole as a registered sex offender. Years later, after watching a show about DNA testing on Court TV, Turner repeatedly petitioned the court that a DNA test be performed on him. The test proved his innocence, and Texas Governor Rick Perry granted Keith Turner a full pardon. The real rapist has not been apprehended.

# Keith Turner

| | |
|---:|:---|
| **INCIDENT DATE:** | December 6, 1982 |
| **WRONGFUL CONVICTION:** | Rape |
| **AGE ENTERING PRISON:** | 22 |
| **AGE LEAVING PRISON:** | 28 |
| **WRONGFUL TIME SERVED:** | 6 years |
| **TIME ON PROBATION:** | 16 years, 1 month, 20 days |

*On parole as a sex offender*

*Exonerated and
visits his mother's grave*

2005

# Mother

The day Keith Turner was exonerated, he went to tell his mother, Doretha Williams.

Twenty-two years earlier, he had been arrested for the rape of a coworker, a thirty-three-year-old mother of three. She claimed to recognize him mainly by the distinct, raspy sound of his voice. Before his arrest, Keith had never been in trouble with the law. He grew up in South Dallas, going to Willow Grove Church with his mother and sister. After graduating from Lincoln High School, he spent almost two years at Texas College in Tyler on a football scholarship.

His mother, a schoolteacher, raised him with an emphasis on education, religion, and family. Today, you can see the honesty and humility from this upbringing in every line and movement of Keith's face. The day he was arrested, his mother stood an inch away from his face and asked him one thing: "Did you do this?"

"No, I didn't," Keith replied.

She could see that he was telling the truth and never questioned him about it again. This exchange would happen several times, with many different people, before justice would come to light.

When Keith was convicted and sentenced to twenty years, he turned and saw his mother sitting behind him in the courtroom. He watched the life fade from her eyes as she slowly shook her head. It must have terrified her, but she was firm with him.

"You can survive," she said. "Lots of people go to prison. I know you didn't rape that woman, but they've found you guilty and you have to be strong and make it through your time."

But Keith didn't feel strong. All he felt was anger, and he was so angry he blamed her. He blamed her for not preventing what happened to him.

He was angry she didn't have the money to hire a better lawyer, hadn't made the police realize they had the wrong man, had not convinced the jury of his alibi—the list went on and on.

She tried to reason with him.

"You're mad at me, but I did what I could. I spent my money. I gave all my money to the lawyer, and they ran over him. There is nothing more I can do. I can't just come down there and tell those people to let you out."

During his first month in Coffield, he didn't write her one single time. He didn't put her on his visiting list, he didn't even tell her which unit he was in, but she never gave up on him. She would have called every unit in Texas to find him if she had to.

Eventually Keith's anger began to fade. He started writing her and allowed her to visit him. Her letters meant the world to him.

"You know when you are behind bars and your mother writes you something, that means a lot. It's not about what she says; it's about the letter. That kind of gives you strength, because if your mother will be strong for you out there, you can be strong for her in here. You gotta be. You gotta be strong for her 'cause that's why she is being strong, so you can make it."

She came to visit him twice before he realized that something was wrong. The third time, she walked into the visiting room slowly, as if each step was a burden and a struggle. Her face had thinned tremendously, and her body looked frail and brittle.

Keith had lost weight too—almost fifty pounds in only two or three months. He forced himself to think that his mother's transformation was merely a result of sleepless nights from the worry and anxiety about his situation. Behind his hope lurked the realization that his mother was really sick.

"She knew she was dying, so she made an effort to come down one last time. She was barely walking. When people get cancer, their face gets small; they get weak and stuff like that. I knew she wasn't all right. I could tell."

He could tell she was dying, but he will never be sure if it was the cancer or the grief that was killing her.

"I didn't know if it was the sickness, or if my case was just running her down. Maybe it was both, just knowing I was here for something I didn't do, and such a bad thing, it just probably wore her down. She just couldn't take no more."

Keith Turner went to his mother's funeral in shackles and handcuffs. While being restrained was humiliating, his attendance was more than most prisoners convicted of

*Doretha Williams,
Keith's mother.*

a violent sex crime are allowed. In fact, he would not have been permitted to be there at all except for the unexpected kindness of a prison officer, Major Michaels. When he called Keith into his office to speak to him the day his mother died, something about Keith's demeanor attracted his attention. The major asked him about his case, and Keith was so convincing that Major Michaels decided to bend the rules and escort Keith to the funeral himself.

The van ride to the funeral was surreal. Keith knew they were going to the church and why, but he was in denial. When his grandmother called the prison to tell him that his mother had passed away, he heard her, but in his heart he didn't believe her. Because his mother was a well-respected and beloved teacher, the sanctuary at Willow Grove Church was full. Keith was grateful to be there, but sitting beside an armed guard who stopped each family member from hugging or touching him made him realize what he had become: the property of the State of Texas.

Major Michaels stood in the doorway of the church listening to every word and every testimonial about Mrs. Turner. When the service ended, Keith was allowed the kindness of going to kiss his mother good-bye. He had to shuffle up to her casket in chains in front of everyone. They lifted the coffin lid, and Keith looked in. Seeing her body, cold and distant, should have convinced him, but he still could not believe she was gone.

He went back to prison, where he kept feeling his mother's protection. After the funeral, Major Michaels took a special interest in Keith. He took him off fieldwork and gave him a good job indoors. Major Michaels said that in over twenty-five years he had escorted a lot of prisoners to funerals, but he had never heard one as moving as Mrs. Turner's, and he had never seen a family that impressed him so much. What he heard that day caused him to take a long, hard look at Keith Turner, and what he saw convinced him he was looking at an innocent man. From that point on, prison life was still never easy, but thanks to his mother, Keith had a friend in high places.

When Keith was released, he was paroled but not exonerated. When he went back to live in his mother's house, he finally accepted the truth that his mother was gone. His first day out of prison he came home to find members of his family gathered in her old house to celebrate his return, but he couldn't join in the festivities. He kept wandering, looking through the closets. Concerned, his grandmother asked what he was looking for.

Keith said, "I'm looking for her."

"Well, she's not here."

Sitting alone on the floor in his mother's bedroom, Keith finally heard and saw and believed that she was gone.

"It took me three hours before I would even go outside to my own welcome-home party."

A lifetime of his mother's lessons had taught him how to live and what kind of man he should be. For the next fourteen years, he was going to need it. He was out of prison, but life as a sex offender—wrongfully convicted or not—is difficult. Each year on his birthday, instead of celebrating, he had to drive down to the Department of Motor Vehicles to get a special driver's license with the words "sex offender" stamped on it. The law required him to carry it at all times, and he hated it.

"I'll tell you what I did. As soon as I got that license, I would not put it in my wallet like I was supposed to. I would stick it in the trunk of my car under the spare tire. That way I had it if a police officer pulled me over, but I was not going to keep it out where anyone could see it."

For fourteen years he bounced between jobs. When he couldn't get anyone to hire him, he drove around picking up scrap metal to make ends meet and to raise the money to send thousands of letters requesting DNA testing. Besides the truck full of scrap, he also carried another burden—guilt. Deep down, Keith felt responsible for his mother's death.

On December 22, 2005, the day he was exonerated, Keith drove to a small cemetery in South Dallas where his mother was buried. He was finally able to tell her it was all over. After twenty-two years of fighting for justice, he could finally say, "You don't need to worry about me anymore, Mom. I'm all right."

But Keith is not all right.

Through the years he has gone to several counselors. One suggested Keith write a letter to his mother, asking for her forgiveness in the hope that this might relieve his guilt.

Keith wrote her this letter.

He can never mail it, but he hopes she will somehow receive it.


*Dear Mother,*

*I miss you. Sometimes I dream about you. You are washing dishes but you still talk to me. I am all alone.*

*When I was growing up, I remember kids at school calling me a "momma's boy." We were so close. You taught me to read, sew, cook, and drive. Your lessons have stayed with me and I follow your advice still. Birthdays were my favorite. Every year you made me a chocolate cake. Boy, do I love your chocolate cake.*

*Thank you. Thank you for helping me. When I got fired from my job at Smith Furniture after the arrest, you helped me every day finding a new job to help with attorney's fees. You worried about me riding the bus because I might get hurt by people angry about the charge against me, so you drove me to work every day and picked me up. Together we paid the attorney, me and you. I remember you came home crying one day because no one in our family would help you with my case.*

*Thank you for coming to court every day, you never left my side. We rode together to court every day, me and you. The moment I was convicted, I turned around to look at you. I could see in your eyes you was hurt, but you knew I was innocent. Thank you for never leaving my side.*

Tested

I am sorry. I am sorry that I blamed you for me being locked up. I know that you spent your money hiring a lawyer for me. I was so angry at the world, and I took it out on you. I didn't write you because I was mad. I don't know why I blamed you. I wonder if being separated from you was more than I could take. Momma, I am still so angry.

I know now that you were sick with cancer during the time of my trial and prison. I now understand why you couldn't get out of the car on a prison visit; the cancer had spread and you were too weak to leave the car. I feel empty. I don't know if I can ever forgive myself. I give you all the credit because even when I was angry and hateful, you still loved me and believed in me. You never gave up on me—to the end.

Do you see me as the man I am today?

Would you be proud of me?

I miss you. I am all alone. It took me a few years after I got out to come visit you. But now I visit you often. I wanted to buy you a headstone, but the cemetery won't let me. They will let me buy you a bench, but I don't want a bench. You deserve a headstone. I make sure you have flowers. I love you, Momma, and I am sorry about what I put you through. You don't have to worry now; I will take care of you. You spent your entire life taking care of me; now I will take care of you.

Momma, all that I have is yours. Even though you aren't here, all I have is yours. If I could trade all that I have for one day with you, I would.

Momma, thank you for teaching me all the lessons I needed to know to survive. I am a good person today because of you. You always told me there would be darkness, but that I would come into the light. You were right. I think about you all the time. I am alone with this burden.

Thank you for being a good mother.

I love you,

Keith

112

Stephen Brodie
Photo by Chad Windham

# Afterword

## *Voice*

The men have changed me.

I am a different person now, a better person, for having the chance to know them and tell their stories. Every moment I spent with them altered my view of the world and demonstrated the resilience of the human spirit. They also taught me that our judicial system is broken and must be fixed. Interviewing Stephen Brodie made me realize this is not just a problem that started before I was born. This is still happening.

We had to go to the Dallas County Jail to interview Stephen Brodie. The artificial light and sterilized odor that just barely covered the stench of sweat—and God knows what else—made me dizzy.

The meeting was surreal.

We sat in a small storage room connected to an office where eight guards sat, working at their computers. My mother wore her clerical collar and sat in front of a large gas mask connected to a tear gas canister, which hung limply from a hook in the wall. I sat in a broken-backed black leather chair next to a pile of chains connected to zip-ties, which serve as modern-day handcuffs and shackles. We briefed the sign language interpreter on Stephen's case history as we waited for him to be brought in.

A guard escorted the prisoner in and stood by the door for the entire interview; Stephen sat down in the chair in front of us. He is a big man, with the pale white skin of someone who hasn't been outside in a long time. His prison uniform was baggy and ill-fitting, with gray-and-black horizontal stripes. I don't know why that surprised me. I have talked to almost all of the men in this book about the uniforms in prison, but something about seeing those stripes on a man I knew was innocent knocked the breath from my body.

The first few moments of our interview were agonizing. Neither my mother nor I had ever worked with the hearing impaired, and our awkwardness was palpable in that small, stuffy room. After floundering through a few questions, my mother finally asked Stephen to describe his life growing up. His silence made him appear shy, but as he signed his answers to our questions, the rapid and emphatic movement of his hands displayed his emotions. At first, hearing his story in the voice of the female interpreter was strange, but as I focused my attention on his face, I began to understand.

Stephen had fetal alcohol syndrome. At eighteen months, he developed spinal meningitis and became deaf. When his mother learned this, she abandoned him at a train station. Eventually a family who had a hearing-impaired daughter adopted him. His new family helped him learn sign language and tried hard to help him as he made his way through the public school system, but to protect him, they probably sheltered him too much.

He rebelled, dropping out of high school three months before he was scheduled to graduate. After leaving high school, Stephen felt lonely and disconnected. He tried to make human connections by joining several churches and going on mission trips to poor areas of Tennessee and Colorado. But soon Stephen committed a crime so petty and almost endearing that it would have been laughable if it hadn't set off a horrific set of events. Stephen was arrested for stealing quarters out of a vending machine at the local swimming pool. When he was brought in for questioning, the first thing the police asked him was, "Where is your hearing aid?"

They then proceeded to interrogate him for eighteen hours, some of that time without an interpreter present. It took a while before Stephen was able to comprehend that they were asking him about something more than a petty theft. They wanted to know about the abduction and molestation of a five-year-old girl who was taken from her bedroom while her parents slept.

Stephen immediately admitted to taking the quarters but kept trying to tell the officers he knew nothing about the little girl. Exhausted and confused after hours of relentless questioning, he finally confessed both to the rape of the child and to an imaginary sex crime that the police officer had simply invented. Almost as soon as the "confession" occurred, Stephen tried to retract it and make the officer understand he was innocent of everything but stealing some change. From that moment on, until he accepted a plea bargain, he maintained his innocence. He questions how anyone ever believed he was the one who actually committed the crime. He asks how a deaf man could break into a house and crawl silently through a window when he couldn't even hear the sounds of his own movements. Although it seems to defy logic, he was charged with the crime.

Stephen eventually took a plea bargain and served five years. He was released on parole but refused to register as a sex offender because he found the whole process confusing and, more importantly, because he knew he was not one. So he has been repeatedly reimprisoned for parole violations. He is now once again back in prison for a crime he did not commit. It doesn't take an interpreter to understand that Stephen has been through hell. The stories of the eleven other men in this book display the horrors of the Texas prison system. How those horrors could ever be navigated and endured by someone who cannot hear or fully speak is beyond imagination.

Finally a letter from Stephen's adoptive father reached the hands of Michelle Moore with the public defender's office, and they agreed to reexamine his case. Combining their work with improved fingerprint technology, they were able to prove his innocence and identify the actual perpetrator, who is a pedophile known to have molested multiple children ranging in age from five to fifteen.

The status of Stephen's case and the timing of his release are still unknown.

All he wants to do is move out to the country, return to the ranch where he once worked, and be with the animals. In the city, people are "bad," and it is too easy to fall under their sway. In the country, he can be with his horses. He doesn't need to be able to hear or speak for them to understand. When he describes the ranch, the boss, and the job he hopes is waiting for him where he can work cattle alongside several other older, hearing-impaired cowhands, it becomes evident that Stephen is a man of surprising talents.

He loves life on the ranch. It's hard work and he's been kicked plenty of times, but it's worth it. He rides, shoes, and breaks horses and can't wait to get back to his two favorite chestnut mares—Diablo and her little sister Baby Gurl—who wait for him in Oklahoma. Asked if he is good with cows, he eagerly signs, "Of course," then unexpectedly adds, "bulls too." He is not only a good ranch hand but also a bull rider with a long list of rodeos he has entered and sometimes won.

Today, Stephen spends his days in the windowless county jail, far removed from the country life he longs for. At night, he dreams of a ranch in Oklahoma, with lots of horses and cows and plenty of trees.

Stephen Brodie will soon be released. His full exoneration is pending.

It seems strange to say that this book is the story of twelve lucky men. Wrongly convicted, they experienced things we cannot even begin to comprehend, but somehow the cries of these twelve men were heard. They have been, or will be, released.

Countless, unimaginable numbers of innocent people still sit in prison and will never be freed.

This must stop.

Peyton Budd

Photo by Chad Windham

Michelle Moore
DNA attorney for the Dallas County Public Defender's Office
Photo by Chad Windham

# A Conversation
# with Michelle Moore

As a public defender for Dallas County, Michelle Moore works with inmates seeking exoneration, reviewing their cases for possible new evidence that could free them.

*Q: How did you get started doing this important work?*

A: I got thrown into the briar patch. When the DNA statute came about in 2001, I was working as a public defender, and the judge whose court I was in says, "I don't want to deal with this. You figure it out." It's a lot of work going through old files and digging up old stuff, so nobody wanted to do it. Eventually I ended up doing it for all of the courts.

*Q: When did you become aware that there was something broken in the criminal justice system?*

A: From the start of my career, I saw wrongful convictions. I saw people withholding evidence that affects these guys' lives, and personal vendettas come up. There were cases where I completely disagreed with the judge or the jury. At first, I didn't realize it was so widespread.

*Q: What are the primary causes of wrongful convictions?*

A: Most of the cases have mistaken eyewitness identity. Show-ups and lineups that were done incorrectly, like Johnnie Lindsey, who's put in a six-person lineup without a shirt on. Or sometimes investigators will do the show-up first and then the lineup, which is kind of Christopher Scott's story. Then there are cases where the police or DA's office was withholding evidence and still does anything to get a conviction.

*Q: A surprisingly large number of these exoneration cases come out of Dallas. Is there something in the Dallas system that's special?*

A: I think it's because Dallas saved the evidence, so when DNA science developed, it was still there and could be tested. They were very proactive, and although we sometimes bash former DA Henry Wade for being controlling and ruthless about getting convictions, at the same time he helped us when it came to evidence. He kept it. So in a strange way, you've got to give him credit.

*Q: Do you think Dallas has more wrongful convictions than anywhere else?*

A: No. In fact, I'd be surprised if when we looked at some of the smaller counties around Texas, we wouldn't see more like these—if they had kept their evidence. But because they didn't, we will never know. In lots of places they have innocent people sitting in prison; everybody knows it and they aren't doing anything about it.

*Q: The cases in this book and the exonerations around the country are mostly rape cases, crimes that typically leave DNA at the scene. From what you have seen, is there the same percentage of wrongful convictions in all the other types of cases that don't have DNA evidence?*

A: Definitely. And I think we're fools if we don't think that.

*Q: How many cases are currently waiting on your desk in Dallas?*

A: Close to four hundred. We've reviewed about forty of them so far.

*Q: Out of forty reviews, how many have proved innocence?*

A: Over twenty.

*Q: If out of every forty you're reviewing, twenty, or half of them, are coming back innocent, what does that mean about how many wrongfully imprisoned people there are in the system?*

A: There's probably thousands. How scary. I get hundreds of requests every week. My desk is unreal. I don't know when I last saw the top of it.

*Q: What about the non-DNA cases?*

A: That's one of the things we are concentrating on right now, but without scientific evidence, non-DNA cases can be a lot more difficult to prove. Many times I'm sitting there looking at it, going, "I don't think this guy did it, but I don't know if we can prove it."

*Q: Out of the twelve men in this book, there are two Anglos, one immigrant, and the rest are African-American. Does that pattern hold true across the cases you see?*

A: You have to remember that in Dallas in the mid-80s to the '90s, there were some assumptions. If there was a cross-racial rape, then I think it was easy to snag a black guy for that. Also, if the suspect had a prior record, he gets on the police's radar screen. In the authorities' minds, this guy is trouble, so when something happens, they go to him first. Often they try to make him the perpetrator of something that's much more violent than anything he has previously shown himself capable of.

  I don't know how to train police, and even the DAs, to prevent this tunnel vision. Just because a suspect did something in the past doesn't mean he made a greater leap in the future. I think it also comes down to not only the tunnel vision but also the way you got promoted. Whether you were a police officer or DA, you weren't going to get promoted if you didn't get convictions. Like the investigator in the Steven Phillips's rape case who set up that crazy lineup where all twenty victims were in the same room. He got detective of the year for his role in that case.

*Q: Are there certain types of evidence that are just not as reliable as we once thought?*

A: Oh, definitely. Eyewitness testimony. It's sad to say, but I've gotten to where I don't pay attention to it anymore; it's just not reliable.

Q: *If someone serves on a jury, what kind of evidence would you tell them to look for or to be suspicious of?*

A: I definitely would question the eyewitness ID. I want to see the science, give me some DNA. I want more than circumstantial evidence. I think it's too easy for everybody to have tunnel vision on circumstantial evidence. So I guess those are the main things.

Q: *What about this job has most challenged your belief in the justice system?*

A: I have trouble with the Brady violations. That's where either the DA or the police department did not disclose evidence that could have proved the defendant innocent. The prosecution should by law have handed it over to the defense in the trial. We've got a lot of that. I have an uncle who's in the DPS [state police], and I've worked with these guys, so I have tremendous respect for the police just as I have enormous respect for the district attorney's office. But it's just disheartening to think somebody didn't hand over exculpatory evidence—it's disheartening to think that there was a win-at-all-costs attitude.

Q: *After these men are released, are their problems over?*

A: Not at all. It's going from one extreme to the other. You go from somebody telling you when to eat, when to go to the bathroom, when to work, when to take your medication to suddenly being responsible for all this stuff, and more. It is such an extreme shift for them. The other difficulty for these guys is after they get out, they're a celebrity for a couple of weeks. They go to all these places, and suddenly it stops, and then there is nothing. Many of those relationships they imagined in prison are changed. Parents aren't there all the time as they thought they would be, or their parents got older or are now in a nursing home. So they have to go see their mother and take care of her. That's not the mom they had when they went in.

Relationships, obviously, are very, very difficult. Even the first day out can be overwhelming. I try to warn them so they will be prepared for that. Suddenly they've got family and friends gathering around them, and they all want a little piece of them. They get overwhelmed.

Then there usually is some female who surfaces somewhere, and it's just hard. These guys don't even know how to function, so that's difficult.

There are lots of little practical things that just all add up. They don't have ID, so we can't get them a checking account. I don't have a Social Security card for them;

they're supposed to start releasing the TDC ID, but that's not enough for us to get a state ID. We have to have a birth certificate, and most of these guys' moms have died, and they usually hold the birth certificate. So we have to order it, which takes more time. If they get paychecks, they can't even cash them without somebody else cashing it for them, because they don't have ID or a checking account.

Q: *Even though some of them will eventually get money as compensation, they don't get it the day they get out. Do they get out with that two hundred bucks and a suit on their back, just like every other Texas parolee?*

A: Oh no, they don't get that at all; they get *nothing*. Unlike a parolee, who gets one hundred dollars and the new suit of clothes the day he leaves the prison, and then another one hundred when he shows up for his first parole visit, these guys get nothing, not even clothes. Any clothes they get are ones we donate. Most of the clothes come from law students.

Q: *One of the guys said that if he had been found guilty and released on parole, a parole officer would be assigned to help him find work. But if you are not guilty, when they set you free, there is no system of support.*

A: Yes, and the problem is about the only job they can find is as a courier, but that means getting your driver's license, and most of them haven't driven in over twenty years. They have to study for a driving test, and even when they get the job they often can't hold it because they get lost. The city has changed so much. Forget about reading Mapsco; that's not going to happen. And they barely know how to use a cell phone.

Q: *So what troubles them most when they get out?*

A: Relationships. In the end, these guys are resourceful, for the most part. So even if they lose money, they usually make it OK because they know how to make it on the streets. But it's the relationships that are so difficult because they want to trust so badly, so the first female they see who says, "Oh, I'm not in it for the money, I love you, I'm here to help you," they trust them. So it's just so difficult.

Q: *What would you say surprises you the most about them?*

A: That they are just so good. Through and through. They've never been spoiled. They're not jaded. They still find wonder in all these little things. The fact that they can go through what they've gone through, and some of it is so horrible for them to talk about, and yet they remain stellar individuals who are so noble. That's what touches me. I just don't know how these guys did it—and they're such honorable men. They're amazing. And these guys are so patient. The guys will sit there and say, "I'm patient, I'm a patient man. I pray every night. I trust that God will find a way."

Q: *If someone wants to learn more about the issues that surround wrongful convictions, where would you tell them to go?*

A: Definitely check out the Innocence Project network; it is a great online source to learn about these cases. They try to keep track of all the innocence cases that come out across the country and are really proactive. It's a good source for people to go to.

Q: *If somebody is in jail or in prison and innocent, what should they do?*

A: If you are in Dallas County, write to me or to Craig Watkins's Conviction Integrity Unit. No matter where you are, don't discount the Innocence Project groups or Centurion Ministries. Write to them. Try to get those guys on board. And just keep at them. Keep hammering them; give them as many details and as much information as possible. The more I know about the case, the more you'll fascinate me with your story. Tell me the truth, tell me a good story, and you're gonna catch me.

Q: *When you feel overwhelmed, what do you hold onto to keep doing this work?*

A: I think about these guys, but also I always say my little prayer, "Let me find out the true story. Let me find out what happened, and if this guy's supposed to walk out, help me to find the truth." I just have to take it one step at a time.

# Peyton Budd

Her combined interests in psychology, writing, and criminal justice led Peyton Budd to the creation of *TESTED*. Selected for the University of Virginia's Young Writers Workshop and for an international studies exchange program in Switzerland, she has published poetry in *Vibrato,* an award-winning literary magazine. Peyton continues her studies at Colorado College where she focuses on writing, literature, psychology, and Arabic.

# Dorothy Budd

A former child sex crimes prosecutor for the Dallas County District Attorney's office, Dorothy Budd has worked as a DA in the Juvenile Division, trying juvenile, domestic violence, and child welfare cases until becoming a felony prosecutor in the Crimes Against Children Division. Reverend Budd also holds a Masters in Divinity from Perkins School of Theology at Southern Methodist University. She now serves as an Episcopal deacon at The Church of the Incarnation in Dallas.

# About the Photographer
## Deborah Luster

**B**est known for the series *One Big Self: Prisoners of Louisiana,* Deborah Luster photographed for six years in Louisiana's prison system, including the state's maximum security prison at Angola. Her work is included in the permanent collections of the San Francisco Museum of Modern Art, the Whitney Museum of American Art, the Los Angeles County Museum of Art, and the Houston Museum of Fine Arts. A monograph of *Tooth for an Eye,* her current project on violence in Orleans Parish, is forthcoming from Twin Palms Publishing. She is represented by Jack Shainman Gallery.